£3

Swami
Vivekananda

An Iconoclastic Asetic

Swami
Vivekananda
An Iconoclastic Asetic

Dr. Ajeet Jawed

Reader, Satyawati College,
University of Delhi

Ane Books India

New Delhi ♦ Chennai ♦ Mumbai ♦ Bangalore ♦ Kolkata ♦ Lucknow

Swami Vivekananda-An Iconoclastic Ascetic

© **Dr. Ajeet Jawed 2007**

Published by

Ane Books India

Head Office	4821, Parwana Bhawan, 1st Floor, 24 Ansari Road, Darya Ganj, New Delhi - 110 002, India, Tel.: +91(011) 23276843-44, Fax: +91(011) 23276863 E-mail: anebooks@vsnl.com, Website: www.anebooks.com
Chennai	Avantika Niwas 1st Floor, 19 Doraiswamy Road, T. Nagar, Chennai - 600 017, India, Tel.: +91(044) 28141554, 28141209 E-mail: anebooks_tn@airtelbroadband.in
Mumbai	G-012, Ground Floor, Jui Nagar Railway Station Building, Jui Nagar (East), Navi Mumbai - 400 706, India, Tel.: +91(022) 64522840, 64522841 E-mail: anebooksmum@gmail.com
Bangalore	38/1, 1st Floor Model House, First Street, Opp. Shamanna Park, Basavannagudi, Bangalore - 560 004, India, Tel.: +91(080) 41681432 E-mail: anebang@airtelbroadband.in
Kolkata	Flat No. 16A, 220 Vivekananda Road, Maniktalla, Kolkata - 700 006, India, Tel.: +91(033) 23547119 E-mail: anekol@vsnl.net
Lucknow	C-26, Sector-A, Mahanagar, Lucknow - 226 006, India, Mobile - +91 93352 29971

ISBN (10) : 81-8052-195-8
ISBN (13) : 978-81-8052-195-9

Printed at Brijbasi Art Press, Noida

Dedicated to

My Teacher **Padma Srivastava**

*(Ex Head of the Department of Political Science
Daulat Ram College)*

University of Delhi

"Upon the banner of every religion will soon be written, inspite of resistance: 'Help and not Fight', 'Assimilation and not Destruction', 'Harmony and Peace and not Dissension"

— **Swami Vivekananda**

Preface

India today is passing through troubled times. Fanaticism, Communalism, casteism, regionalism, linguism and crisis of character have reached a new high. Religion and religious leaders are being used by the obscurantist forces to spread hatred and hostility and to attain legitimacy of their nefarious designs. One such victim of theirs is Swami Vivekananda. A great son of Mother India, he infused a new strength in our freedom struggle and ignited a passionate devotion in the hearts of his countrymen for the liberation of their motherland and for the construction of a better world.

He was an iconoclast who refused to follow the traditional norms set for ascetics. He gave a new interpretation to religion, a new definition of patriotism and sought to build a new social order based on the principles of equality, freedom and fraternity. The message to he imparted is not for a particular community or related a particular religion it is for the entire world community. In his own words:

"I have a message and I will give it after my own fashion. I will neither Hinduise my message, nor Christianise it, nor make it any 'ise' in the world. I will only my-ise it and that is all."

For this work, considerable research has been done. I have relied mainly on Vivekananda's writings, speeches, letters and his extempore conversations. I have also looked at memoirs, newspaper reports, magazines along with numerous books written on the swami by his disciples and both Indian and foreign writers.

I acknowledge my gratitude to the authorities and staff of National Archives Library, Nehru Memorial Library, Central Secretariat Library, Central Reference Library, Delhi University, Delhi Public Library and Lala Hardayal Library for providing facilities for my research work. I am grateful to my colleague Ms. Victoria for reading the manuscript and Amarjeet Kaur and Saroj Rajdan of Delhi University Central Reference Library who helped me with books. I also express my gratitude to my husband M A Jawed and little Aryan whose cooperation made my work easier.

Ajeet Jawed

Contents

Swami Vivekananda: The Man in the Making

"He is not a pond, he is a reservoir. He is not a pitcher or a jug, he is a veritable barrel. He is not a minnow or sardine; he is a huge red-eyed carp. He is not an ordinary sixteen-petalled lotus–he is a glorious lotus with a thousand petals."

— Sri Ramakrishna

Vivekananda is one of the greatest sons of India and a chief architect of Indian renaissance. He was a great patriot, prophet and a philosopher who thought and worked not only for political liberation of the country but also for rescuing the teeming millions of the country from social and economic exploitation. His writings, speeches and activities made him a legend in his life-time. His brilliant advocacy of Indian spiritualism in the World Parliament of Religions made him a renowned figure not only in India but the world over.

He was born on 12th January 1863, in a Kayastha family in Calcutta. His real name was Narendranath Datta. His great-grandfather, Ram Mohan Datta, started life as an associate and managing clerk of an English solicitor during the early days of the East India Company's Bengal office and had amassed a large fortune. The mansion he built in Gour Mohan Mukherjee Lane still stands as a reminder of the great patriot monk who was born in that family. Narendranath's grandfather, Durga Charan Datta, however did not follow in his father's foot-steps. Though well versed in Persian and Sanskrit and skilled in his father's profession of law, he renounced the world and became a monk at the age of 25, soon after the birth of his son Bisvanath. He never returned to his family. Durga Charan's wife Shyama Sundri, was a learned poetess, she wrote a collection of poems— Ganga Bhakti Tarangini. Narendranath inherited the art and love for poetry from her. He started writing poems very early in his life and later used this medium to express his spiritual and political ideas.[1]

Bisvanath Datta, father of Narendranath was brought up by his mother. He joined the legal profession and became a well-known attorney of the Calcutta High Court. He was secular to the core and followed the composite Indo-Islamic culture. Though, he did not join any on-going reform movements, he was a supporter of reforms concerning women and encouraged his son to join social reform organisations and movements. Bisvanath's liberal and progressive ideas greatly influenced Narendranath and shaped his outlook. Narendranath's mother Bhuvneshwari Devi was a traditional Hindu lady.[2] Unlike Bisvanath, Bhuvneshwari Devi, was deeply religious, she taught her children the essentials of Hinduism and gave them a deep-rooted understanding of culture by telling them stories from Ramayna, Mahabharta and other holy scriptures. She also made them familiar with other religions, like Islam. Bhupendranath Datta, brother of Narendranath writes, 'From our mother we heard about the fight of Karbala and used to weep and sigh on hearing the tragic fates of Hassan and Hussein.[3] Narendranath was deeply attached to his mother and often spoke with a sense of deep indebtedness. "It is my mother", he declared "who has been the constant inspiration of my life and work."[4]

---

1. Vivek Bhattacharya, *The Spirit of the Indian Culture-Saints of India*, Metropolitan, N.D. 1980, p-492. Also see The Life of SwamiVivekanands; Vol-I, p-2
2. *The Life of Swami Vivekananda,* by Eastern and Western Disciples, Advaita Ashram, Calcutta,1912, 1979 p-20. Vol-I
3. Bhupendranath Datta, *Swami Vivekananda, Patriot and Prophet,* Navabharat Press Calcutta, 1954, p-103.
4. Swami Vivekananda kept contact and took care of the financial problems of his family even in his monastic life. His friend and disciple, Raja of Khetri, Ajit Singh used to send Rs 100/- every month to his family. During the last years of his life whenever Vivekananda was in Calcutta, he would go himself to his mother but if perchance he could not go to her, she would herself come down to Belur to see him and take his advice on family matters. He also took her to pilgrimage.

In his childhood, young Vivekananda heard stories about his grandfather's renunciation of the worldly life and becoming a monk. This perhaps made him curious and inclined towards asceticism. The sight of wandering monks thrilled him and when they would come to his door for alms he used to give them whatever he found at home. To prevent him giving too much to the monks, his family would lock him in a room. Vivekananda wrote later: "When I was only two years old, I used to play with my syce at being a vairagi, clothed in ashes and kaupina. And if a sadhu came to beg, they would lock me upstairs to prevent me giving too much away. I felt that I was also this, and for some mischief I had had to be sent away from Shiva. No doubt my family increased this feeling, for when I was naughty they would say, 'dear dear! so many austerities, yet Shiva sent us this demon after all, instead of a good soul! Or when I was very rebellious, they would empty a can of water over me, saying Shiva, Shiva! And then I was alright always."[5]

He was always restless and it was difficult to control him. As a child he needed constant attention and the Dattas had to have two nurses to keep an eye on him.[6] At the age of six he was sent to school but he stopped going to school, as he did not like the school atmosphere. A private tutor was engaged to teach him. However, he was very intelligent, argumentative and assertive and had extraordinary sense of self-hood. When he was just fourteen years old, his father had to shift from Calcutta to Raipur. Vivekananda's disciples mention an episode in his biography which shows traits of his overpowering personality.

"Many noted scholars visited his father. Naren would listen to their discussions and occasionally joined them. In those days he sought and demanded intellectual recognition from everyone. So ambitious was he in this respect that if his mental powers were not given recognition, he would fly into a rage, not sparing even

5. Nivedita, Sister, *The Master as I saw him*, Udbodhana, office, Calcutta, 1910, p-198.
6. Life of Swami Vivekanand, Vol-I, p-97-98

his father's friends and nothing short of an apology would quiet him. Of course, the father could not sanction such outbursts and reprimanded the boy, but at the same time, in his heart he was proud of his intellectual acumen and keen sense of self-respect of his son." [7]

Narendranath was fearless and used to retaliate sharply if someone hurt his self-dignity. Bhupendranath Roy writes in his book entitled 'Nivedita' one such incident:

"It is said that while still an adolescent he chanced to come to a park where a Christian missionary was giving a lecture. Immediately he saw Swamiji (Naren), he cried 'I see the devil staring in my face.' Without a second's thought Swamiji retorted, 'Yes, you have a mirror before you."[8]

He was brave and many times even in childhood demonstrated his courage. His biographers mention many incidents of young Narendranath saving lives of others while risking his own.[9] Even in his post-monastic life, unlike most men of religion, he never hesitated in exhibiting courage which, was exceedingly youthful and masculine. Once when accosted by two particularly uncivil Christian missionaries on a ship, the Swami held them by the collar and threatened to throw them overboard.[10] Sister Nivedita, his disciple narrated an incident which occured in England, the Swami while travelling across some fields in the company of two English friends—one of them a lady—was assailed by a mad bull which came tearing towards them. The Englishman ran away, but the lady sank to the ground, exhausted by her attempt at running. The Swami at once planted himself between the bull and the lady and escaped sure death only by the bull turning away at the last moment.[11]

7. Ibid., p-41.
8. Bhupendranath Roy, *Nivedita*, Pub- S. Mahto, Bengal year of Pub- N.M, p-37.
9. Life, Vol-I, p-24, 38.
10. Life, Vol-II, p-161. Calcutta, 1979 (Reprint)
11. These are many such incidents. See for detail life of Vivekananda by his Eastern & Western disciples. Vol-I, p-28-29

True to his name, which means chief of men, Narendranath had leadership qualities in his blood. As a child his favourite pastime was playing king, becoming the king everytime they played. He had well-built body made stronger with his training in wrestling and lathi-playing. Some of his disciples from Madras, affectionately addressed him as 'Pahalwan Swami.'[12]

He was rational and had an irresistible desire to know the truth. Nothing discouraged or daunted him. Along with his friends he would very often climb the tree of a neighbour's garden, swing violently from a branch with his head thrown downward. To discourage Naren and his friends the neighbour told them that the tree was haunted by a hobgoblin (a *Brahmdaitya*) and it would break the neck of those who would not desist from acrobatics in his garden. Naren's friends asked him to let go but Naren told them that his neck would have been long off, had there been an iota of truth in the ghost story of the neighbour. Much later he told his disciples: *"Do not believe a thing because you read in a book! Do not believe a thing because another has said so! Find out the truth for yourself! That is realization!"*[13]

Do not believe a thing because you read in a book! Do not believe a thing because another has said so! Find out the truth for yourself! That is realization!

Young Narendranath displayed immense curiosity in watching the world around him. He had a great zest for life, enjoyed organising dramas, gymnastics and magic lantern shows, and was constantly out, seeing interesting places in Calcutta. When he became a monk, he travelled not only in India but also many countries of the world.

In 1871 Naren was admitted to the Metropolitan Institute, founded by Pt. Ishwar Chandra Vidyasagar. There he passed the entrance examination and a year later joined the General Assembly's Institution from where he graduated with an arts degree in 1884.

In his student days, Naren was easily distinguished from others. He was a popular figure both in school and college and was known for his knowledge and oratory

12. Life, Vol-I, p-35, 368.
13. Life Vol-I, p-81.

skills. Once a teacher was going to retire from Ishwar Chandra Vidyasagar's school, who was very popular among the nationalist leaders. The farewell function was to be presided over by the greatest orator of the country, Surendranath Banerjea. Narendra was asked by the students to represent them, he agreed readily. Before the learned all-India leader, Narendra spoke for more than half an hour. That was his first public speech. Much later, Surendranath Banerjea recalled this incident and said that he had heard many eminent orators of world fame but none as Swami Vivekananda.[14]

He had very sharp memory and could recite word by word the text taught in class. Narendranath had a remarkable thirst for knowledge. He was a voracious reader of newspapers, magazines, novels, Indian history and contemporary writings. It was during his college days that he read Herbert Spencer's philosophy but was not fully convinced, he wrote to Spencer criticizing certain points. The author wrote back, appreciating Narendra and with a promise that the ideas in question will be modified in the future edition.

His teachers considered him a genius. Prof WW Hastie, who was his teacher in philosophy and also the Principal of the General Assembly' Institution spoke of him as: "Narendranath Datta is really a genius! I have travelled far and wide, but I have never yet come across a lad of his talent and possibilities, even in the German Universities, amongst philosophical students. He is bound to make a mark in life."[15]

In college, he got interested in theatre and played the role of a yogi in *Nava-Brindavan* of Babu Keshub Chandra Sen, the great social reformer. His physical beauty was superb: stoutly built, he had an intellectual forehead, pearly white teeth, thick, wavy black hair, and a deep musical voice. Vishwananth, who himself was a

> Narendranath Datta is really a genius! I have travelled far and wide, but I have never yet come across a lad of his talent and possibilities, even in the German Universities, amongst philosophical students. He is bound to make a mark in life.

---

14. Ibid., p-45.
15. Ibid., p-48.

lover of music, arranged the services of two well-known musicians—Ahmad Khan and Beni Gupta to train Narendera in music—he turned out to be an accomplished singer. Narendranath's musical skill made him a much sought after figure in all social gatherings. Writing about him Swami Gambhirananda says: "He sang in a sweet baritone, and could play on various instruments with considerable skill."[16] He used to sing at school, college, as well as at Brahmo Samaj meetings. On the occasion of his first meeting with Parmahansa Ramakrishna, Vivekananda was asked to sing. He did so, with the result that his future master passed into an ecstasy. Besides he could swim, row and had a passion for horses and was considered an arbiter of fashion.[17]

A fellow student, Brajendranath Seal, later a famous scholar and educator, wrote about him:

"He was undeniably a gifted youth, sociable, free and unconventional in his manners—an excellent singer, the soul of the social circle; a brilliant conversationalist, though somewhat bitter and caustic, piercing with shafts of wit the shows and mummeries of the world-sitting in the scorner's chair but hiding the tenderest heart under the mask of cynicism—altogether, an inspired bohemian but possessing what bohemian lack—an iron will."[18]

Indeed he was a bohemian very much given to fun and frolic and this astonished even his western disciples. He ate meat, enjoyed drinks, cigars, pepper, chilli, tobacco, pan, supari, ice-creams and attended musical concerts, freely moved with female devotees and made no secret of it. Sister Christine writes in her reminiscences: 'It is true that we were conventional and proper to the point of prudishness. Still even one more bohemian might have been disconcerted. He, in the days when men did not smoke before ladies, would

It is true that we were conventional and proper to the point of prudishness. Still even one more bohemian might have been disconcerted. He, in the days when men did not smoke before ladies, would approach, and blow the cigarette smoke deliberately into one's face.

16. Ibid., p-43, Also see Modern Review, Nov, 1968, p-833.
17. Ibid., p-35.
18. Ibid., p-107.

approach, and blow the cigarette smoke deliberately into one's face." [19]

He did not follow the code of conduct set for the monks nor behaved like one. He often indulged in talking frivolities with his friends in United States. When reminded that he was a monk and should not joke and laugh like an ordinary man, he would reply 'we are children of bliss, why should we look morose and sombre'?[20]

He was straight forward and remained so throughout his life. He didn't claim to posses supernatural powers. In April 1901 he went to Dacca and stayed at Jatin Babu's house. One day a rich prostitute came to see him with her mother. She told him that she was suffering from Asthma and begged him to give some medicines to cure her. Vivekananda expressed his sympathy and replied: 'See here Mother! I am too suffering from Asthma and have not been able to cure myself. I wish I could do something for you'.[21]

As an all-rounder, he left his mark wherever he went and his carefree nature won him friends everywhere. He loved cooking and used to make dishes for his friends and later disciples as well.

He took keen interest in the socio-political affairs of the country, particularly of Bengal. The Brahmo Samaj movement seriously affected him. He read the writings of Raja Rammohun Roy and was greatly inspired by his dynamic personality and liberal outlook. He hailed the Raja as "the first man of new regenerate India."[22] Roy's acceptance of Vedanta, his preaching of patriotism and the love that embraced mussalman equally with the hindu, in all things he claimed himself to have taken up

19. *Reminiscences of Vivekananda*, by Eastern & Western Disciples Advaita Ashram, Calcutta 1961, p-197, 299.

20. *Complete Works* of *Swami Vivekananda*, Advaita Asharm Mayavati Almora, Vol-VI, 1956, p-463.

21. Mrs. Johnson, one of his foreign disciples, left him as she thought that Vivekananda's sickness belied his holiness. Modern Review, March 1969, p-219.

22. Datta, p-7.

the task that the breadth and foresight of Rammohun Roy had mapped out.[23] He came in contact with Debendra Nath Tagore, Keshab Chandra Sen and Pandit Siva Nath Sastri. Their zeal for social reforms particularly regarding caste, attracted him and he acquired the membership of the Samaj and regularly attended its meetings and listened to the addresses and sermons of the Brahmo leaders.[24] Naren's joining the most radical faction of the Brahmo movement linked him to the use of reason against superstition, magic and miracles. Besides, he learnt that the universal religion was practical and entailed to the service of the mankind, and second to preach 'universal theism' not only to the educated classes but also to the uneducated classes and to raise the status of women and the masses. He was also active in Adi Brahmo Samaj's 'Band of Hope'.[25] Naren had also joined the Freemason's Lodge in Calcutta at his father's urging. Freemasonry in India concerned itself with equality, social reforms, philanthropy and a 'common denominator approach to religious unity'. It was another force in the drive towards breaking the caste system, communalism and dietary laws.[26] Pt. Ishwar Chandra Vidyasagar, at whose school, Vivekananda had studied and later taught for a month was another source of inspiration. "After Ramakrishna, I follow Vidyasagar! He exclaimed only two days before his death..."[27]. Vidyasagar's pride in being Indian, his zeal of social reforms, particularly concerning women deeply influenced him. Keshab's advocacy for India's development and Surenderanath's agitational politics impressed him. Bankim Chandra's *Anand Math*, published in 1882, captured his mind and inculcated in him a fiery patriotic fervor.

---

23. C.W. Vol-VII, 1947, p-341.
24. Life, Vol-I, p-202.
25. George M. Williams *Swami Vivekananda*, in *Religions in Modern India*, ed. By Robert-D, Baird, Manohar, 1989, p-318-21.
26. Ibid., p-321.
27. *Vivekananda in Indian Newspapers 1893-02*, ed. By Sankri Prasad Basu & Sunil Bihari Ghose, Pub-Bookland Calcutta, 1969, p-274.

Since childhood he had a longing to see God. His intelligence didn't let him accept the existence of God without he himself seeing Him. This desire took him to Maharishi Debendra Nath Tagore, a prominent spiritual leader and later to Ramakrishna. Initially, he was disappointed and decided not to visit Ramakrishna, his future Master, but the destiny had something else in store. In 1884, his father suddenly died of heart attack, followed by his sister's suicide as a result of a unhappy marriage. The financial problems faced by his family and the failure to get a suitable job affected his sensitive mind. The relatives, who were dependent on his father, became the worst enemies of his family. Perhaps all this was enough to drive him back to Ramakrishna to find God and question Him about the injustices faced by him and his family.

Swami Ramakrishna changed the course of his life. He assured Narendra that the financial needs of his family will be taken care of, Narendra became his disciple and stayed in the *Math*. Brajendra Nath Seal who was Narendra's senior in college wrote about Narendra's transformation under the influence of Ramakrishna's teachings:

"I watched with intense interest the transformation that went on under my eyes. The attitude of a young and rampant Vedantist–cum Hegalian–cum Revolutionary like myself towards the cult of religious ecstasy and Kali worship may be easily imagined; and the spectacle of a born iconoclast and free thinker like Vivekananda, a creative and dominating intelligence, a tamer of souls himself caught in the meshes of what appeared to me an uncouth, supernatural mysticism, was a riddle which my philosophy of the Pure Reason could scarcely read at that time."[28]

He fell under the spell of Swami Ramakrishna's magnetic personality and broader outlook. Ramakrishna, a disciple of Saint Tota Puri had both hindu and muslim disciples. Towards the end of 1866,

---

28. Life, Vol-I, p-172.

Ramakrishana was influenced by Islam. He had his initiation in Islam by Gobind Rai, a hindu a but by follower of Islam chaice. Ramakrishana then started dressing, dining, praying and behaving like an orthodox muslim. He went on repeating the name of Allah and reciting Namaz regularly like a muslim devotee. He used to explain to his disciples: "I have practised all religions: Hinduism, Islam, Christianity and I have also followed the paths of different hindu sects…I have found that it is the same God towards whom all are directing their steps, though along different paths. Wherever I look I see men quarreling in the name of religion—Hindus, Mohammedans, Brahmins, Vaishnavas and the rest but they never reflect that He who is called Krishna, is also called Shiva, and bears the name of primitive Energy, Jesus and Allah as well as the same Rama with thousand names…"[29] He was of the opinion that a mussalman was absolutely as accessible to the divine grace as any child of the Aryan race. Vivekananda was greatly influenced by the catholicity of Ramakrishna's ideas and outlook. He explained later about his Master as;

"To proclaim and make clear the fundamental unity underlying all religions was the mission of my Master. Other teachers have taught special religions, which bear their names, but this great teacher of the nineteenth century made no claim for himself. He left every religion undisturbed because he had realised that, in reality, they are all part and parcel of the one eternal religion."[30] Besides, the humanism of his Master also appealed to him. Ramakrishna regarded all men as the children of the same god and loved them equally. He practiced, what he preached. "O, my Mother, make me the servant of the Pariah (the outcaste), make me feel that I am even lower than the Pariah"

The Master was deeply impressed by his young disciple. He once remarked about Narendera: "He is not a pond, he is a reservoir. He is not a pitcher or a jug,

> He is not a pond, he is a reservoir. He is not a pitcher or a jug, he is a veritable barrel. He is not a minnow or sardine; he is a huge red-eyed carp. He is not an ordinary sixteen-petalled lotus-he is a glorious lotus with a thousand petals."

29. Vivekananda in Indian Newspapers, p-399.
30. Nivedita, *The Master As I saw him*, p-76.

he is a veritable barrel. He is not a minnow or sardine; he is a huge red-eyed carp. He is not an ordinary sixteen-petalled lotus-he is a glorious lotus with a thousand petals."[31] And on another occasion the master said, "Narendra is not a twig floating in a river-the twig that sinks even if a bird alights upon it. Rather he is great tree-trunk, carrying men, beasts and merchandise upon its chest."[32] Swami Ramakrishna spoke prophetic words, which proved true. He said; " You will do great things in the world; you will bring spiritual consciousness to men, and assuage the misery of the humble and the poor."[33] Swami Ramakrishna passed away on August 15,1886 leaving about a dozen of his monk disciples with Narendranath as their head. The young monks devoted themselves to meditation, studied and practised spiritual exercises. Besides Ramakrishna, Buddha's teachings too acquired a hold on his mind. He regarded Lord Buddha, the sanest philosopher, the world ever saw and used to quote him heavily in his teachings and addresses.[34]

Narendra stayed in the monastery until 1890, then he undertook a long tour of India. He was a monk in action and not a monk in meditation. With his shaven head, *gerrua* (saffron) robe and begging bowl, he moved from one place to another. When a question was asked about his *gerrua* robe, he replied "because this is the garb of the beggars! Poor people ask me for alms if I wear white clothes, and being a beggar myself I do not have at most times even a single pie with me to give them. And then it causes me pain to have to refuse one who begs from me. But seeing my gerrua cloth, they understand that the man is a beggar even as one of them, and they would not think of begging from beggars."[35] He met people of different regions, religions and castes but realized that all were victims of

31. *The Gospels of Shri Ramakrishna*, Pub-Ramakrishna Mission, p-793.
32. Ibid., p-542.
33. Modern Review, Nov. 1968, p-834.
34. C.W. Vol-III, 1948, p-529.
35. Ibid., p-131, Vol-II, 1970.

exploitation–social, economic and political. He also witnessed unity in diversity.

When he arrived at Cape-Comorin, he did not have a single paise to pay for a seat in the ferryboat to the shrine. Inspite of the numerous sharks he plunged into the ocean and swam to the temple. On reaching the shrine he fell prostrate in ecstasy before the Goddess. And there, sitting on the stone, he passed into eternal meditation.[36] Independent India paid homage to Vivekananda by constructing a memorial on the rock called V. Mandupam, on which a bronze statue of Vivekananda has been erected.

During two and half years of wandering, he devoted almost one year to the studies of the vedas under Pandit Sankar Pandurang, a great vedic scholar in Pore Bunder, Western India. His wide knowledge of Sanskrit grammar, acquired earlier at Jaypore, stood him in good stead. Pandit Pandurang was charmed with his talented young student and said that India needed a person of the Swami's calibre to interpret Hindu culture and religion in foreign lands. Possibly he had heard about the Parliament of Religions at Chicago. However, Vivekananda did not pay any serious thought to the suggestion and continued his march. Travelling alone as a mendicant, he met people of all grades from common masses to kings, many became his disciples. Among them were Maharaja of Ramnad (Madras) and Maharaja of Khetri.[37] Vivekananda met the Raja of Khetri in June 1891 and stayed with him for five months at a stretch. The Raja had not studied but had great thirst for knowledge. During his stay at Khetri, Vivekananda taught him lessons in Physics, Chemistry and Astronomy and established a small laboratory in the top-most room of his palace, which consisted of

---

36. Ibid., Vol-II, p-203.
37. Raja of Khetri was a great admirer of Mughal rulers particularly of Emperor Akbar. The Raja died of a fall from Sikandara, the tomb of Akbar. He was repairing the tomb at his own expense at Agra and one day while on inspection, he missed his footing and it was a sheer fall of several hundred feet.

necessary instruments and chemicals. He also got the Raja to purchase a powerful telescope, which was installed on the roof of the laboratory, through which he used to show his royal disciple the movement of the stars at night and gave him practical lessons in Astronomy. Raja was a good *Vina* player. He used to play the instrument and often Vivekananda used to sing.[38]

On the request of his disciples, Vivekananda decided to attend the Parliament of Religions, to be held in Chicago in 1893 as a representative of Hinduism. It is at this time that he assumed a new name— Vivekananda.[39] The Parliament of Religion was scheduled to sit on 11th September. He had no money and no friends in that most expensive land which was completely new to him. Moreover he carried no credentials as a delegate to the Parliament. But all these hurdles could not stop Vivekananda. "The cyclone made its way; the dynamite shattered all obstacles."[40] At the Parliament of Religions' Indian delegates were—Majumdar of the Brahmo Samaj, Nagarkar of Bombay, Mr. Gandhi represented the Jains and Mr. Chakravarti represented Theosophy with Mrs. Annie Besant. The Hall of Columbus in the Art Institute of Chicago was packed to capacity with some 4,000 people, eager to hear the representatives of the ten chief religions of the world. While the keen audience was familiar with Catholicism, the Greek Church, Protestantism, and Judaism, it looked forward to learning something new from Islam, Hinduism, Buddhism, Taoism, Confucianism and Zorasterianism.[41]

Popularity of Vivekananda commenced from his very first speech on hinduism. Clothed in a dazzling robe of red silk and wearing the yellow turban he started by addressing the Americans as "Brothers and Sisters of America" which were never uttered by any

The cyclone made its way; the dynamite shattered all obstacles.

---

38. Benishankar Sharma, *Swami Vivekananda* Calcutta 1963, p-19, 20.
39. Life, Vol-II, p-258. Modern Review, Nov. 1968, p-835.
40. Modern Review, Jan 1960, p-57.
41. Ibid., Feb 1969, p-137.

speaker, the effect was electric. There arose a spontaneous peal of applause, which went on for several minutes. Audience was enthralled by his speech and wanted to hear him again and again. The Parliament sat from 11th September to 27th. During this fortnight, Swami's hold over a section of American influential society was firmly established. He became so popular that the organizers "used to keep Vivekananda until the end of the programme to make people stay till the end of the session"[42]

Dr. Annie Besant, the leader of the Theosophists from India, who was also present there, wrote long after:

"A striking figure, clad in yellow and orange, shining like the sun of India in the midst of the heavy atmosphere of Chicago, a lion head, piercing eyes, mobile lips, movements swift and abrupt—such was my first impression of Swami Vivekananda, as I met him in one of the rooms set apart for the use of the delegates to the Parliament of Religions. Monk, they called him, not unwarrantably, but warrior monk was he, and the first impression was of the warrior rather than of the monk, for he was off the platform, and his figure was instinct with pride of country, pride of race—the representative of the oldest of living religions...He brought her message, he spoke in her name, and the herald remembered the dignity of the royal land whence he came. Purposeful, virile, strong, he stood out, a man among men, able to hold his own."[43]

Many American newspapers that wrote about the Parliament, specifically praised Vivekananda's ideas and oratory. He was hailed "an orator by Divine Rights".

Francis Albert Doughty, reporting to the Boston Evening Transcript' from Chicago stated:

"Vivekananda's address before the Parliament was broad as the heavens above us, embracing the best in all religions, as the ultimate universal religion—charity to

42. Life, Vol-I, p-42.
43. Ibid., p-312.

all mankind, good works for the love of God, not for fear of punishment or hope of reward. He is a great favourite at the Parliament, from the grandeur of his sentiments and his appearance as well.. If he merely crosses the platform he is applauded..."[44] The reason for this instant popularity were many. First, he was the youngest of the speakers; barely thirty years of age, attractive and handsome by the Western standard. Second, he spoke English with such fluency and elegance as was not heard usually from platforms and pulpits. Third, his wits, fineness of expression, intellectual agility were unparalleled. Fourth, the burden of his speech was cosmopolitan and not sectarian.

He was ranked as a "Prince among men". Life size pictures of him were pasted in the streets of Chicago with the words "The Monk Vivekananda." "Cyclone has shaken the world"[45] New York Herald spoke of him "undoubtedly the greatest figure in the Parliament of Religion." It also wrote "After hearing him one feels how foolish it is to send missionaries to this learned nation."[46] The Daily Chronicle wrote:

"From the day the wonderful Professor delivered his speech, which was followed by other addresses, he was followed by a crowd wherever he went. While going in and coming out of the building, he was daily beset by hundreds of women who almost fought with each other for a chance to get near him and shake his hand... The Professor seemed surprised at this homage, but he received it graciously enough until it became tiresome from repetition and then he made his entries and exits at times when there were no crowds of women in the vestibule and corridors."[47]

The popularity and fame also brought Vivekananda perhaps the toughest period of his life. His true exposition of Indian Spirituality annoyed and angered

44. *Vivekananda in the Indian Newspapers*, p-2.
45. Ibid., p-305.
46. Ibid., p-305, 240.
47. Ibid., p-4.

the American missionaries who lived on the fat squeezed out of the conversion machinery of Indian heathens, as conversions had its commercial side; the religious embassies in India were terribly expensive organisations. Till then American people knew only the darker side of India. That Indians were uncivilised; that they strictly observe inhuman customs like throwing their first child in the jaw of the crocodiles, killing the girl child, burning the widow alive on the funeral pyre of their dead husbands, voluntary killing beneath the wheels of the "Jagarnath's Chariot", on polygamy, caste inequalities and so on. Dozens of such books narrating these features among others were published. One such book was entitled "India and its Inhabitants" written by Mr. Caleb Wright. This illustrated book was published in 1858 in 353 pages. It ran into seven editions in two years and as many as 36,000 copies were sold.[48] A poem written by a missionary in India, entitled "Songs For The Little Ones At Home" had been included in the nursery rhymes of the land. It stated:

> "See that heathen mother stand
> Where the sacred current flows;
> With her own maternal hand
> Mid the waves the babe she throws.
> "Hark! I hear the piteous scream;
> Frightful monster seize their prey,
> On the dark and bloody stream
> Bears the struggling child away
> Fainter now and fainter still,
> Breaks the cry upon the ear;
> But the mother's heart is steel
> She unmoved that cry can hear.
> Send, oh send the Bible there,
> Let its precepts reach the heart;
> She may then her children spare-
> Act the tender mother's part."

---

48. Modern Review, Jan 1969, p-58, 59.

The fervent appeal for sending the Bible to India was also backed by other arguments. Are not the womenfolk there caged like parrots? Are not numerous children hung on trees in baskets to be eaten by birds? Is not this barbarous land full of fearful tigers, cunning priests, jewel-bedecked dancing girls and voluptuous native princes?[49] Pandita Ramabai Sarsawati's book "The High Caste Hindu Women" written in 1887, contained ghastly tales of Indian women, which greatly strengthened the arguments and advocacy of the missionaries.[50] Thanks to the misdoing of these missionaries, such calumnies were so widespread that at every meeting the Swami was challenged with a few of these stock charges. Vivekananda countered their viewpoint and thus created a sensation among the Americans. He had the courage to express his views frankly even when it earned him displeasure and wrath of the missionaries. He made the Americans familiar with the brighter side of India, its rich heritage of spirituality and culture, with the result that many enlightened millionaires of US who had heard Vivekananda, stopped the pecuniary support to the missionaries. Thus angered, the missionaries consequently gave circulation to many unfounded stories about Vivekananda.[51]

Theosophists were his second opponents, although Theosophy was of American origin, at the end of the nineteenth century it took roots in South India. Before leaving for America, Vivekananda requested a letter of introduction from Col. Olcott. He promised one readily on the condition that Vivekananda join their association—Vivekananda's refusal resulted in anger. The Theosophists, though numerically few in America, joined forces with Christian missionaries— Vivekananda was called an imposter. When reports of Vivekananda's penury reached Madras, an important

49. *Swami Vivekananda in America-New Discoveries* Marie Louise Burke, Advaita Ashram, Calcutta, 1958, p-143.
50. Pandita Ramabai was an Indian scholar. She got converted to Christianity in England and accepted Professorship at Cheltenham College.
51. *Vivekananda in Indian Newspapers*, p-214.

member of the Order wrote to his American friend, "The scoundrel will die soon; we are saved by the grace of God."[52] His popularity made the Brahmos jealous too. Majumdar of Brahmo Samaj called him a cheat. Vivekananda wrote to Ala Singa in anger and anguish:

"Majumdar slandered me to the missionaries in the Parliament, saying that I was a nobody, a thug, a cheat, and he accused me of pretending to be a monk. Thus he greatly succeeded in prejudicing their minds against me. He so prejudiced President Barrows that he did not speak to me decently."[53] However, Vivekananda single handedly fought with his opponents and won, this victory not only made him popular but also led India to glory.

His magnetic charm won him admirers and followers from all over America. Women were particularly impressed with his demeanor and good looks, 'I thought of him as a God of Greek sculpture' writes a particularly impressed admirer, 'he was dark of skin of course and had large eyes which gave the impression of midnight blue'. To educated upper-class American women Vivekananda was indeed the lateral sensation, many women sought to marry him. It is also said that a heiress approached him and proposed but Vivekananda declined saying, "he was a Sanyasi and all women were as his mother!"[54] John Davison Rockfeller, the richest man of America met him and donated enormous sums of money to finance public institutions.[55] He spent three years in United States, undertaking whirlwind tours lecturing on Vedanta and other issues related to India, he spoke not as a religious saint but as a representative of India. His views were considered fatal to the orthodox beliefs. The intelligentsia admired him, heard him attentively, invited him to lecture at the Harvard University, and even offered him the Chair of Oriental Philosophy in

---

52. Modern Review, Jan 1969, p-58.
53. *Life*, Vol-I, p-181-82.
54. Ibid., p-318.
55. *Swami Vivekananda in America*, p-123.

recognition of his merit. He helped many students at Harvard University with the philosophical problems they were encountering during the course of their study.[56]

He started the first Vedanta Society in New York in 1896. The work of spreading the Vedanta philosophy was entrusted to Swami Kripananda, a russian jew named Leon Landsberg. Vivekananda initiated him.[57] His disciples wore the same turban as the Swami.[58] A book containing his lecture notes, entitled 'Raja Yoga' was published, it was received enthusiastically by the American intelligentsia and ran into three editions within few weeks of publication.

Americans were greatly impressed by this unique universalist. They expressed their feelings in the following words:

America thanks India for sending him, and beg her to send many more like him

"America thanks India for sending him, and beg her to send many more like him; if such there are, to teach by their example those of her own children who have not yet learnt the lesson of universal fraternity and openness of mind and heart; and by their precepts those have not yet come to see Divinity in all things and a oneness transcending all."[59]

From America, he proceeded to England. Though his stay there was only for three months, he made a great impression on the thoughtful people who came in contact with him. The famous ecclesiastic Rev. Canon Willberforce held a levee to honour him. "It was indeed a rare sight" remarked the London correspondent of the Indian Mirror, "to see some of the most fashionable ladies...seated on the floor cross-legged, of course for want of chairs, listening with all the *bhakti* (devotion) of an Indian *chela* (disciple) towards his *guru* (teacher)"[60] There he delivered lectures in many gatherings including a conference of the London Hindu Association wherein The

56. Ibid., p-519.
57. *Life*, Vol-II, p-412. Modern Review, March 1969, p-213.
58. Raja of Khetri had taught him wearing turban.
59. *Vivekananda in Indian Newspapers*, p-13.
60. The Indian Mirror, June 25, 1896.

Hon. President of the Association, Dadabhai Nauroji was also present.[61] He also met Max Muller, the celebrated Indologists.[62] He was called the Hindu *Yogi*. A daily Paper "The Standard" wrote: "Since the days of Raja Rammohun Roy, with the single exception of Keshub Chandra Sen, there has not appeared on an English platform a more interesting Indian figure than the Hindu who lectured in Prince Hall."[63] England gave him three disciples, GG Goodwin, Miss Margaret Noble (Nivedita) and Mr and Mrs Savier. He also visited Switzerland, Italy and France.

On his return to India, he received a hero's welcome. At Ramnad, the Raja of Ramnad devoutly joined his people in driving the state carriage, carrying the Swami and later erected a monument on the spot where he landed.[64] The swami had no time to rest on his laurels, he undertook a whirlwind tour, carrying the message of resurgent spirituality, strength and fearlessness to remote parts of India. These addresses, later published under the title of 'Lectures from Colombo to Almora', did much to restore the self-confidence of Indian intellectuals, to awaken the masses and to stimulate the youth of India.

He founded the Ramkrishna Mission with headquarters at Belur, near Calcutta, on May 1, 1897. The aim of the misson was not only for spreading vedanta but also the service of the suppressed and the sufferer without any distinction of race, religion or region. Vivekananda himself became the General Secretary of the Mission.[65] Bi-weekly journals,

---

61. *Reminiscences of Vivekananda, p-289.*
62. Max Muller was a German Professor and Sanskrit Scholar. He settled down in Oxford and remained there till he died in 1900. His services were hired by the East India Company to edit a series of publications entitled the Sacred Books of the East.
63. *Life*, Vol-II, p-413.
64. Manmohan Ganguly, *Swami Vivekananda-A Study* Contemporary Pub, Calcutta, 1907, p-43.
65. Modern Review, July 1969, p-518.

Brahmavadin and *Prabuddha Bharta* (Awakened India) in English, were started from Madras to awaken the masses. A year later, he started a Bengali magazine, the *Udbodhan* from Calcutta. In the same year, he visited Lahore where he met Tirthram Goswami, then a Professor of Mathematics, who was so impressed by Vivekananda that he renounced the world and was later known as Swami Rama Tirtha, and subsequently preached Vedanta both in India and America. Swami Sivananda was sent to Ceylon the same year.[66] In June, 1899 during his second visit to USA, a second Vedanta Society was started in San Francisco. In 1900 Vivekanand attended the Congress of Religion in Paris and travelled across many countries before his return to India by the end of the year. His health was failing, he was suffering from diabetes and asthma. He passed away on July 4, 1902, at the young age of 39 years, 5months and 24days.

Hindus, Muslims, Sikhs and Christians alike in India and abroad paid rich tributes to him. He had shown them a path where all could walk together, work together, towards building a new world in which mankind could live in true fraternity. His ideas still inspire and will keep on inspiring as long as there are conflicts on the issues of religion, exploitation of poor and domination of the powerful and the subjugation of the weaker.

---

66. *Vivekananda in Indian Newspapers, p-607.*

Social Ideas

"Come be men kick out priests who are always against profress"

— **Swami Vivekananda**

Vivekananda wanted to change the entire social system by eradicating all evils and to reconstruct it on the principles of equality, freedom and fraternity. He declared "To the reformers I will point out, I am a greater reformer than any one of them. They want to reform only little bits. I want root and branch reform."[1] Social ideas of Vivekananda were the product of his family background, his association with Pt. Ishwar Chandra Vidyasagar, the Brahmo Samaj, his rational outlook, scientific education, study of vedanta and empirical knowledge of men and things over large part of the globe.

Vivekananda's upbringing was greatly responsible for inculcating in him a rational outlook. Bisvanath, his father was an unorthodox man and had a large circle of friends and clients belonging to different castes and communities. They used to visit their house for social and official purposes. Debates, discussions, arguments, counter arguments would be made on various issues in such meetings. In this liberal and literary atmosphere young Vivekananda learnt the art of reasoning.

Besides by nature he was non-conformist and did not submit to social rules and practices blindly even in his childhood. He used to question the rational and validity

---

1. Swami Vivekananda, *Lectures from Colombo to Almora*, Advaita Ashram, Almora, 1947, p-127. Also see C.W. Vol-III, 1948, p-213.

behind such practices and many a times violated them to see the consequent effects. His disciples write in his biography that even as a boy, Vivekananda did not follow caste-rules.

"There used to come to Naren's house many clients of his father for consultation. They were of different caste and creed. There were separate hookas kept for them. Naren in the absence of his father used to enter into the parlour and try the hookas of the separate castes and creeds. But the Mohammed an hooka was his favourite He used to take whiff from each and every one of them. When he was caught by his father he asked him 'O father why, I was trying to see what would happen if I broke the caste!' When reprimanded, he would say 'I cannot understand what difference it can make."[2]

Pt. Ishwar Chandra Vidyasagar also made a lasting impression on young Vivekanand's mind. Vidyasagar's zeal for social reforms had made him popular among the progressive people not only in Bengal but all over India. He fought against polygamy, child marriage, prohibition of widow marriage and sought moderniza- tion by introducing English along with Sanskrit in his institution. He was proud of Indian culture and refused to accept English ways which was the norm of the day with the well-educated Bengali gentlemen. Vivekananda's social ideas witness the profound influence of Vidyasagar.

Vivekananda was also greatly influenced by Brahmo Samaj. It was set-up by Raja Rammohun Roy, who, in the first quarter of 19th century started a powerful social reform movement. In his zeal for eradicating in-human social practices, he was helped and supported by the English authorities in Bengal. However, after the end of the East India Company's rule, the new rulers—for the maintenance and consolidation of their rule—aligned with the orthodox sections of the Indian society and gave up the socially progressive policy of the Company.

> O father why, I was trying to see what would happen if I broke the caste!' When reprimanded, he would say 'I cannot understand what difference it can make.

---

2. Life, Vol-I, p-23.

The intellectuals in Bengal led by Keshab Chandra Sen resented this attitude. Keshab Chandra Sen formed Brahmo Samaj of India in 1866 and spearheaded the social reform movement. Vivekananda in his student days joined Keshab's group and later its splinter radical group, Sadharn Brahmo Samaj headed by Pt. Sivanath Sastri. Like brahmo leaders, Vivekananda too condemned casteism, don't touchism, rigidity of the kitchen rules, priesthood, superstitions, and enslavement of women.[3]

In school and later in college, Vivekananda was known for his radical views. His scientific and secular education had further strengthened his rational outlook. In debates and discussions, he never minced words in criticizing orthodox practices being followed without reasoning. He refused to accept the theory of Varna i.e., the four Varnas were the creation of Brahma. His disciples mention an episode in this context in his biography. Once a friend of Vivekananda was ordered by his father to salute a Brahmin. The boy who belonged to the caste next to the Brahmin caste, asked his father "Why one must salute the Brahmins?" father replied, "My boy, Brahmins have come out from the mouth of Brahma, the Creator". Unconvinced with the explanation, the boy went to Vivekananda and asked him why God should have created such great differences and distinctions. Vivekananda made a revolutionary statement. He said, "It is all foolishness. The thing is, you see, a method by which one class tyrannises over the others and profit thereby in all the ways."[4]

Why one must salute the Brahmins?

When he became a monk, he became more outspoken about social evils and advocated total overhauling of the social system. He disagreed with the reforms carried out in the past and the then going on reform movements. He declared:

"Most of the reforms that have been agitated for during the past century have been ornamental. Everyone of these reforms only touches the first two

---

3. Ibid., p-56.
4. Ibid., p-137.

castes and no other... Every effort has been spent in cleaning their own houses. But that is no reformation. You must go down to the basis of the thing, to the very root of the matter. That is what I call the radical reform. Put the fire there and let it burn upwards and make an Indian nation."[5] Of all the social evils, Vivekananda regarded caste-system and the enslavement of women responsible for the backwardness of the hindu society. He said:

"What can you expect from a race which for hundred years has been busy in discussing such momentous problems as whether one should drink a glass of water with the right hand or the left? What more degradation can be than that the greatest minds of a country have been discussing about the kitchen for several hundred years, discussing whether I may touch you or you touch me and what is the penance for the touching."[6]

In his lectures, letters and writings he criticized caste-based inequalities and atrocities, made it known to the people that caste was the creation of the priest and had nothing to do with religion.

He condemned the priests for degrading a large number of hindus as shudras by imposing caste system.

> If the Shudra hears the Vedas, fill his ear with the molten lead and if he remembers a line, cut his tongue out. If he says to the Brahmin, 'You Brahmin' cut his tongue out, a diabolical old barbarianism.

"If the Shudra hears the Vedas, fill his ear with the molten lead and if he remembers a line, cut his tongue out. If he says to the Brahmin, 'You Brahmin' cut his tongue out, a diabolical old barbarianism."[7]

"...I am pure and all the rest are impure! A beastly, demonic, hellish religion this."[8]

Wearing the mask of religion, the brahmins cunningly exploited the beautiful shudra women and cleverly included them in their circle, and also the genius born from shudra parentage, thereby depriving the shudra of the wisdom. Digging at the ancient Indian history, he explained.

5. C.W. Vol-III, p-216, 217.
6. Ibid., p-271.
7. *Lectures from Colombo to Almora*, p-219.
8. *Letters of Swami Vivekananda*, Advaita Ashram, 1946, p-251.

"By this very qualitative caste-system which obtained in India in ancient days, the shudras class was kept down bound hand and foot. In the first place, scarcely any opportunity was given to shudras for the accumulation of wealth, or the earning of proper knowledge and education; to add to this advantage, if ever a man of extraordinary parts and genius were born of the shudra class, the influential higher sections of the society forthwith showered titular honours on him and lifted him up to their own circle. His wealth and the power of his wisdom were employed for the benefit of the alien caste-and his own caste-people reaped no benefit of his attainments; and not only so, the good for nothing people, the scum and refuse of the high castes, were caste-off and thrown into shudra class to swell their number."[9] He also cited a few names in this context:

"Vasistha, Narada, Satyakama, Jabala, Vyasa, Kirpa, Drona, Karna and others of questionable parentage were raised to the position of Brahmin or Kshtriya in virtue of their superior learning or valour; but it remains to be seen how, by uplifting, the prostitute, maidservent, fishermam or the charioteer class was benefited."[10]

Blaming Shankra for the unjust system, he said:

"The movement of Shankra forced its way through high intellectuality; but it could be of little service to the masses, because of its adherence to strict caste-laws, very small scope for ordinary emotions, and making Sanskrit the only vehicle of communication...He had no liberality. How he has defended that the non-Brahmin castes will not attain to supreme knowledge of Brahmin!...' He could not adduce from Vedas that the Shudras should not study the Vedas.

"And what specious arguments! Referring to Vidura (uncle of Pandava brothers and a most saintly character,

9. C.W. Vol-IV, 1948.
10. Ibid.,

considered to be an incarnation of Dharma.) he has said that he became a knower of Brahma by reason of his Brahmin body in the previous incarnation. Well, if nowadays any shudra attains the knowledge of Brahma, shall we have to side with your Shankra and maintain that because he had been Brahmin in his previous birth, therefore he has attained to this knowledge? Goodness! What is the use of dragging in Brahminism with so much ado? And such was his heart that he burnt to death lots of Buddhist monks-by defeating them in argument! And the Buddhists, too were foolish enough to burn themselves to death, simply because they were worsted in argument! What can you call such an action on Shankra's part except fanaticism.?[11]

He not only condemned the caste-system but did not observe the caste rules himself, and never made secret of this non-conformism. His biographers mention many such occasions where Vivekananda publicly flouted caste-norms:

"On the way, while going to Brindaban, Vivekananda noticed a man smoking Chillum of tobacco comfortably by the wayside. He was weary and worn and so he asked the man to let him have a little smoke. The man almost dropped his Chillum with horror as he belonged to the lower caste. "It would defile you, Sir! I am a bhangi, a sweeper", he said. When Vivekananda heard this, his instinct rebelled, and he went on his way. Hardly had he gone half-a-mile when the thought came throbbing 'What! I who believe in the Oneness of all life, I who abandoned all ideas of caste and distinction to be so bound down by the spirit of Don't-Touchism! Shame on me that I fell back from smoking the Chillum of tobacco from his hands as soon as heard, he was sweeper! Ages of instinct!" The thought made him so restless that he turned back and found the man still seated there. He sat down beside him and said "my son, do prepare me a Chillum of tobacco.' This time Vivekananda did not listen to his plea that he was an outcaste. Being cheered

11. C.W. Vol-VII, 1947, p-116, 118.

up by Vivekananda and made to feel that he indeed was a brother, the man did as he was asked. Joyous at heart for having overcome a lifelong samskara, Vivekananda satisfied his desire and continued his journey".[12]

During his travel through Central India, he lived with a family of a sweeper caste and many a times took food cooked by them. Vivekananda told one such incident to his disciples:

"In the course of my wanderings, I was in a certain place where people came to me in crowds and asked for instruction. Though, it seemed almost unbelievable, people came and made me talk for three days and nights without giving me a moment's rest. They did not even ask me whether I had taken any food. On the third night when all these visitors had left, a low-caste poor man came up to me and said 'Swamiji, I am much pained to see that you have not taken any food these three days. You must be tired and hungry. Indeed, I have noticed that you have not even taken a glass of water'. I thought that Narayana Himself had come in the form of this low caste-man to test me. I asked him 'Can you give me something to eat? The man said 'Swamiji' my heart is yearning to give you food, but how can I give you Chapatis baked by my hands. If you allow me I shall be glad to bring you flour, lentils, and other things, and you may cook them yourself.' At that time, according to the monastic rules, I did not touch fire so I told him, 'You had better give me the Chapatis cooked by you. I will gladly take them.' Hearing this the man shrank in fear; he was a subject of Rajah of Khetri and was afraid that if the latter came to hear that he, a cobbler, had given Chapatis to a Sanyasin, he would be severely dealt with and possibly banished from the state. I told him, however, that he need not fear and that the rajah would not punish him. He could not believe me. But out of the kindness of his heart, even though he feared the consequences, he brought me the food having cooked himself. I doubted at that time whether

12. Life. Vol-I, p-217.

it would have been more palatable if Indra, the king of devas, should have a cup of nectar in a golden basin before me. I shed tears of love and gratitude and thought, 'Thousands of such large-hearted men live in lowly huts, and we despise them as low-castes and untouchables."[13]

Vivekananda's predecessor, Swami Dayananda a well-known reformer from Gujarat, vehemently opposed eating food from the hands of the low-caste people. He said that the persons belonging to the higher caste should not eat food prepared by a shudra as their characteristics would enter the body and mind of the higher caste person.[14] Vivekananda characterized this as hypocrisy and irreligiousness on the part of the higher-castes and pointed out that the low-caste people were the real body of the society. It is through their physical labour the influence of the brahmin, the prowess of the kshtriya and the fortune of the vaishyas are possible and yet they are treated in an inhuman way.[15]

He strongly opposed untouchability and regarded it as a mental disease. He warned its supporters: "There is a danger of our religion getting into the kitchen. We are neither Vedantists, Puratanies nor Tantrists, we are just 'Do not touchists.' Our religion is in the kitchen. Our God is the cooking pot, and our religion is 'don't touch me, I am holy.' If this goes on for another century, everyone of us will be in a lunatic asylum.[16]

"Monks and Sanyasins and Brahmins of a certain type have thrown the country into ruin. Intent all the while on the theft and wickedness, those pose as preachers of religion! They will take gifts and at the same time cry, 'Don't touch me.[17]

'Don't touch', Don't touch' is the only phrase that plays on their lips! How mean and degraded has our

> Monks and Sanyasins and Brahmins of a certain type have thrown the country into ruin. Intent all the while on the theft and wickedness, those pose as preachers of religion! They will take gifts and at the same time cry, 'Don't touch me.

---

13. Life. Vol-II p-214.
14. Swami Dayananda Saraswati, *Satyartha Prakash*, English translation by Durga Prasad, Jan Gyan Prakashan, N.D. 1970, p-366.
15. C.W. Vol-III. p-168
16. Ibid. Vol-III, p-167.
17. Letters, p-251.

eternal religion become at their hands! Wherein does our religion lie now? In Don't touchism, alone, and nowhere else."[18]

Again as admonition, he said:

"Aye in this country of ours, the very birth place of vedanta, our masses have been hypnotized for ages. To touch them is pollution, to sit with them is pollution, hopeless they were born, hopeless they must remain! And the result is that they have been sinking, and have come to the last stage to which a human being can come. For what country is there in the world where man has to sleep with the cattle?"[19]

You are continually telling them don't touch me! Don't touch this or that! Is there any fellow feeling or sense of Dharma left in the country? Kick out all such degrading usages! ...Know this for certain, that no great work can be done by that body one limb of which is paralyzed."[20]

Lambasting his co-religionists, for the humiliations a low-caste had to face and hypocrisy on the part of the higher-castes, Vivekanand said:

"Was there ever a sillier thing before in the world than what I saw in Malabar country? The poor Pariah is not allowed to pass through the same street as the high-caste man, but if he changes his name to a hodge-podge English name, it is alright; or to Mohammed an name it is alright. What inference would you draw except that these Malabaris are all lunatics, their homes so many lunatic asylums...[21]

To what a ludicrous state are we brought! If a Bhangi comes to anybody as Bhangi, he would be shunned as the plague, but no sooner does he get a cupful of water poured upon his head with some mutterings of prayers by a padri, and get coat on his back no matter how

---

18. C.W. Vol-V, p-23, 1947.
19. C.W. Vol-III, p-167.
20. Romain Rolland, *The Life of Swami Vivekananda and the Universal Gospel*, Advaita Ashram, Calcutta 1931, p-165.
21. C.W. Vol-II, 1970, p-294-95.

threadbare and come into the room of the most orthodox Hindu—I don't see the man who then dare refuse him a chair and a hearty shake of the hands! Irony can go no further."[22]

He regarded Brahmins as the enemy of Hinduism— their atrocities perpetrated on the lower-castes forced the latter to leave the Hindu fold. Expressing his eye-witness account of the situation in southern India, Vivekananda stated:

"And come and see what they, the padris are doing here in Dakshin (south) They are converting the lower classes by lakhs, and in Travancore, the most priest ridden country in India—where every bit of land is owned by Brahmins....nearly one-fourth has become Christians! And I cannot blame them, what part have they in David and what in Jesse?"[23]

In his travels abroad he noticed the prevalent social equality, freedom and a sense of fraternity in the western societies. This made him more vocal about his opposition to the social inequalities in Indian society. In a letter to his Brahmin disciple Alasinga Perumal from Yokohama on 10th of July 1893, he wrote:

"Come, see these people and then go and hide your face in shame. A race dotards, you lose your caste if you come out! Sitting down these hundreds of years with an ever increasing load of crystallized superstition on your heads, for hundreds of years spending all energy upon discussing the touchableness or untouchableness of this food or that, with all humanity crushed out of you by the continuos social tyranny of ages- what are you?"[24]

On his return to India, Vivekananda along with his like-minded disciples made efforts to make the people aware that caste was not sanctioned by the real religious books and non-observance of the caste-rules did not mean the violation of hinduism. In *Prabudha Bharata* (1898), he declared:

---

22. *Lectures from Colombo to Almora*, p-218.
23. Ibid., p-18.
24. Letters, p-64.

"We (the swami and his disciples) refuse entirely to identify ourselves with Don't-touchism' That is not Hinduism, it is in none of our books, it is an orthodox superstition which has interfered with national efficiency all along the line.[25]

It is in the books written by the priests that madness like that of the caste are to be found and not in books revealed from God.[26]

We believe that nowhere throughout the Vedas, Darshanas or Puranas or Tantras, it is ever said that the soul has any sex, creed or caste.[27]

Aye, let every man and woman and child, without respect of caste or birth, weakness or strength, hear and learn that behind the strong and the weak, behind the high and low, behind everyone, there is that infinite soul, assuring the infinite possibility and the infinite capacity of all to become great and good."[28]

Reflecting on the failure of all the movements from Buddha to Raja Rammohun Roy, he said:

"Failure! Beginning from Buddha down to Rammohun Roy, everyone made the mistake of holding the caste to be a religious institution, and tried to pull down religion and caste all together, and failed. But inspite of all the ravings of the priests, caste is simply a crystallized social institution which, after doing its service, is now filling the atmosphere of India with its stench, and it can only be removed by giving back to the people their lost social individuality."[29]

In his lectures, Vivekananda referred to Guru Nanak, Chaitanya and Kabir who believed in the equality of human beings and preached brotherhood. He asked his countrymen to follow their teachings and shun narrow thinking:

> It is in the books written by the priests that madness like that of the caste are to be found and not in books revealed from God.

---

25. C.W. Vol-V, p-226.
26. C.W. Vol-VI, p-395.
27. Letters, p-90.
28. C.W. Vol-III, p-193.
29. Life, I, p-530.

"Each Hindu I say, is a brother to every other, and it is we who have degraded them...And so the whole country has been plunged to the utmost depth of meanness, cowardice and ignorance. These men have to be lifted; words of hope and faith has to be proclaimed to them. We have to tell them that you are also like us and you have the rights that we have.[30]

If God is in me, why should I accept the indignities of the world? Rather it is my business to abolish them."[31] Advising those who wanted to work for reforms, Vivekananda said:

"If you wish to be a true reformer, three things are necessary. The first is to feel. Do you really feel for your brothers? Do you really feel that there is so much misery in the world, so much ignornce and superstition? Do you really feel that men are really your brothers? Does this idea come into your whole being? Does it run with your blood? Does it tingle in your veins? Does it course through every nerve and filament of your body? Are you full of that idea of sympathy? If you are, that is only the first step.... One more thing is necessary. What is your motive? Are you sure that you are not actuated by greed of gold, by thurst of fame or power? Are you really sure that you can stand to your ideals, and work on, even if the whole world wants to crush you down?...Then you are a real reformer.."[32]

Citing a saying in Bengal, Vivekananda suggested to the brahmin that he should like the cobra, suck the poison he had injected in the social body to cure it, failure of which would lead to disastrous consequences:

"Beware Brahmins, this is the sign of death! Arise and show your manhood, your Brahminhood, by raising the non-Brahmins around you—not in the spirit of a master—not with the rotten canker of egotism crawling with superstitions and the charlatanry of the East and the West—but in the spirit of a servent."[33]

> If God is in me, why should I accept the indignities of the world? Rather it is my business to abolish them.

> Beware Brahmins, this is the sign of death! Arise and show your manhood, your Brahminhood, by raising the non-Brahmins around you—not in the spirit of a master—not with the rotten canker of egotism crawling with superstitions and the charlatanry of the East and the West—but in the spirit of a servent."

30. *Inspired Talks with Vivekananda*, Advaita Ashram Almora, 1946, p-94.
31. Ibid.,
32. C.W. IV, p-155.
33. C.W. IV, p-300.

He praised the role of the kshtriyas who in his views had contributed greatly in fighting against the priestly tyranny and in the development and democratization of the hindu society.[34] He also appreciated the Muslim and the British rule for weakening the caste-system. He said "Even to the Mohammed an rule we owe that great blessing, the destruction of the exclusive privilege".[35]

Materialism brought in by the Britishers too was playing a positive role as it had "come to rescue of India in a certain sense, by throwing open the doors of life to everyone, by destroying the exclusive privileges of caste by opening up to discussion the inestimable treasures which were hidden away in the hands of very few..."[36]

He expressed the hope that under the then existing capitalist system, caste system will disappear. "No religion is now necessary to kill it (caste). The Brahmin, shopkeeper, shoemaker and wine-distiller are common in Northern India. And why? Because of competition. No man is prohibited from doing anything he pleases for his livlihood under the present government, and the result is neck to neck competition, and thus thousands are seeking and finding the highest level they are born for, instead of vegetating at the bottom."[37] However, Vivekananda did not favour the abolition of the caste. He sought to eliminate its ugly and inhuman feature i.e., the degradation of people on the basis of the caste, birth as the criteria of the caste and restricting certain avenues for particular castes. Caste according to him was a social institution and social grouping in the society was a natural order. Besides, he was not against expertise of a profession linked with a particular group. He opined:

"It is in the nature of society to form itself into groups and what will go will be these privileges! Caste is a natural order. I can perform one duty in social life,

34. C.W. IV, p-273.
35. C.W. III, 1948, p-294.
36. Ibid, p-157.
37. Letters, p-76.

and you another; you can govern a country, and I can mend a pair of old shoes but that is no reason why you are greater than I, for can you mend my shoes? Can I govern the country? I am clever in mending shoes, you are clever in reading Vedas, that is no reason why you should trample on my head; why if one commits murder should he be praised and if another steals an apple why should he be hanged? This will have to go."[38]

He did not favour leaving the hereditary profession. While answering a question in this context asked by a disciple, he said:

"Even with the awakening of knowledge, the potter will remain a potter, the fisherman a fisherman, the peasant a peasant. Why should they leave their hereditary calling? Don't give up the work in which you are born, even if it be attended with defects...If they are taught in this way, why should they give up their respective callings? Rather they will apply their knowledge to the better performance of the work to which they have been born. A number of geniuses are sure to arise from among them in course of time."[39]

Vivekananda gave a new interpretation to the concept of varna. He said that all men are equal and at a different time exhibit the qualities of four varnas:

"As there are sattva, rajas and tamas-one or the other of these gunas more or less in every man, so the qualities, which make a Brahmin, Kshatriya, Vaishya or a Shudra, are inherent in every man, more or less. But at times one or the other of these qualities predominates in him in varying degrees and is manifested accordingly. Take a man in his different pursuits, for example when he is engaged in serving another for pay, he is in shudrahood; when he is busy transacting some piece of business for profit, on this account, he is a Vaishya, when he fights to right a wrong then the qualities of a Kshatriya come out in him; and when he meditates on God, or passes his time in conversation about him, then

---

38. *Lectures from Colombo to Almora* p-161.
39. C.W. Vol-VII, 1947, p-150.

he is a Brahmin. Naturally it is quite possible for one to be changed from one caste into another. Otherwise, how did Vishvamitra became a Brahmin and Parshuram, a Kshatriya?"[40]

Thus he emphasized over caste-mobility. One could change his caste by acquring the necessary qualities. He said birth is nothing, the environment is everything. None is good or bad because of the caste he belonged to. Everyone has the capacity to be what one wants. The monopoly of education by a handful of men had led to the ruin of the country. It was time to disperse it among the masses.

"Teach the masses in the Vernaculars, give them ideas; they will get information, but something more is necessary. Give them culture... The only way to bring about levelling ideas of caste is to appropriate the culture, the education, which is the strength of the highest castes."[41]

He said that it was sheer selfishness to deprive the low-caste people from acquiring education:

"Liberty is our natural right to be allowed to use our body, intelligence or wealth according to our own will, without doing any harm to others; and all the members of the society ought to have the same opportunity for obtaining wealth, education or knowledge...Those who say that if the ignorant and the poor be given liberty, i.e., full right to their body, wealth etc., and if their children have the same opportunity to better their condition and acquire knowledge as that of the rich and the highly situated, they would be perverse-do they say for the good of the society, or blinded by their selfishness?[42]

For the luxury of a handful of the rich, let millions of men and women remain submerged in the hell of want and abysmal depth of ignorance, for if they get wealth and education, society will get upset!

> For the luxury of a handful of the rich, let millions of men and women remain submerged in the hell of want and abysmal depth of ignorance, for if they get wealth and education, society will get upset! Who is society? The millions, or you, I and a few others of the upper classes?

---

40. C.W. Vol-V, 1947, p-128-29.
41. *The Hindustan Review*, Feb. 1903, p-145.
42. Letters, p-424.

Who is society? The millions, or you, I and a few others of the upper classes?"[43]

The solution to the caste problem according to him was not in bringing down the higher but by raising the lower. He advocated not equal but more opportunities for the Shudras saying, "If the Brahmin has more aptitude for learning on the grounds of heredity than the Pariah, spend no money on the Brahmin's education, but spend all the money on the Pariah...if the Brahmin is born clever, he can educate himself without help...This is justice and reason as I understand it."[44]

In order to break the compartmentalization of the hindu society, he like the Brahmo Samaj leaders also suggested inter-caste marriages between the castes and subdivisions of the castes so that they might draw closer to each other. Vivekananda advised:

"Learn good knowledge with all devotion from the lowest caste. Learn the way to freedom, even if it comes from the Pariah, by serving him. If a woman is jewel, take her in marriage even if she comes from a low family of the lowest caste."[45] Here his ideas were contrary to Swami Dayananda who opposed inter-caste marriages.[46]

For the overall development of the society, Vivekananda advised Indians to visit foreign countries and to remodel their society by incorporating good elements of the social structure of the west.

"No man, no nation...can hate others and live; India's doom was sealed the very day, they invented the word Malechha and stopped from communion with others.[47]

I am thoroughly convinced that no individual or nation can live by holding itself apart from the community of others and whenever such an attempt has

No man, no nation...can hate others and live; India's doom was sealed the very day, they invented the word Malechha and stopped from communion with others.

43. Ibid.,
44. C.W. Vol-III, p-193.
45. Ibid., p-132.
46. *Satyartha Prakash*, p-150.
47. C.W. Vol-V, p-41.

been made under false ideas of greatness, policy or holiness-the result has always been disastrous to the secluding one."[48]

Vivekananda's exhortations for the reconstruction of the society—in the light of the reason and the real spirituality—were revolutionary in nature and naturally created a stir in the hindu society. For the ignorant and uneducated classes he was a Masiha, a monk besides being highly educated. His words carried weight among the masses. The progressive praised him but the orthodox hindus particularly the brahmins bitterly attacked him. Swami's open denunciation and non-observance of caste rules aroused so much anger that they castigated him saying, Vivekananda is a cheat, a fraud and as a non-brahmin had no right to adopt the sanyasin garb. They also started his character assassination, accusing him of drinking, and eating beef while in America. When Vivekananda came to know this, he sharply reacted:

"...do not try to boss me with your nonsense. Do you mean to say that I am born to live and die as one of those caste-ridden, superstitious, merciless, hypocritical, atheistic cowards that you find among the educated hindus. I hate cowardice. I will have nothing to do with cowards.."[49]

He wrote further:

"If the people in India want me to keep strictly to my Hindu diet, please tell them to send me a cook and money enough to keep me. This silly bossism without a mite of real help makes me laugh."[50]

He also made it known to the brahmins that "Brahmins were as much a mix race as the rest of the mankind and that their belief in their racial superiority was largely founded on fiction."[51]

Fearless as he was he moved forward on the path he had designed for himself. He boldly declared in

---

48. C.W. Vol-IV, p-10, 1948.
49. Letters, p-243.
50. Ibid.,
51. Life, Vol-I, p-247.

Margin notes:

...do not try to boss me with your nonsense. Do you mean to say that I am born to live and die as one of those caste-ridden, superstitious, merciless, hypocritical, atheistic cowards that you find among the educated hindus. I hate cowardice. I will have nothing to do with cowards..

If the people in India want me to keep strictly to my Hindu diet, please tell them to send me a cook and money enough to keep me. This silly bossism without a mite of real help makes me laugh.

Brahmins were as much a mix race as the rest of the mankind and that their belief in their racial superiority was largely founded on fiction.

London on July 18, 1896 that he would abolish caste in drinking and eating, establish civil marriage, and allow widows to remarry, do away with infant marriages and expunge all restriction on foreign travel.[52]

On his return he faced the warth of the orthodox hindus, they raised a big hue and cry against his exhortations that shudras had the same right to religion and that they too could be initiated. His association with the western people was resented, they did not like him teaching vedas to the people of west, his eating with the european disciples too was opposed, and on this account he was driven out of a private temple.[53]

Despite condemnations, Vivekananda continued with his onorthodox ways. On the birth anniversary of Swami Ramakrishna he invested the holy thread to 50 disciples.[54] He continued flouting caste-rules publicly. Sister Nivedita writes that she herself witnessed the Swami breaking caste and religion based barriers in Punjab and Benaras. He called Mussalman vendor, bought and ates sweetmeats from his hands.[55]

He warned his countrymen to shun narrow ideas and outlook and stop fighting among themselves as independence was round the corner "I see that the independence of India will come in some unthinkable way but if you cannot make yourself worthy of it, it will not live over three generations. India cannot be Japan or Russia. She must stand on her own ideal. She will have to build up a government that includes members of all castes, with no superiority complex between them."[56] His popularity increased with each passing day. He became a Prophet for the Indian youth, a role-model and a torch-bearer who illuminated their minds and infused a spirit for fighting inequalities based on birth and caste.

---

52. *Vivekananda in Indian Newspapers,* p-105.
53. C.W. Vol-VIII, 1959, p-136.
54. C.W. Vol-VII, p-108.
55. *The Master As I Saw Him,* Nivedita, p-93.
56. Lizelle Reymond, *The Dedicated*-Biography of Nivedita, The John Day Company, New York, p-953, p-182.

WOMEN EMANICIPATION

Vivekananda was deeply concerned with the plight of the Indian women. In his opinion, ill treatment of the women was one of the greatest sins of India. For the progress of the country and the society, upliftment of womenfolk was essential.

In those days women were considered inferior to men and were denied rights and liberties enjoyed by men. They were confined to houses and their duty was to rear and bear children and to serve the family. They were denied education and were dependent on others for survival. There was a deep rooted social prejudice against women' education. It was believed that if they were educated, some or the other calamity will befall-widowhood being one. Besides, it was considered fit for dancers and unbecoming of the modest. They were also subjected to inhuman customs and practices. Although Raja Rammohun Roy had succeeded in rescuing women from the practice of sati, their condition remained unchanged. The early influence of ideas and ideals Raja Rammahun Roy, Ishwar Chandra Vidya Sagar, Keshab Chandra Sen, the Brahmo Samaj, played an integral part in forming Vivekanands' ideas on women emancipation. His sisters suicide impressed on his mind the desperate situation of women. Vivekanandas' scientific outlook study of Vedanta too convinced him that all were equal, irrespective of the gender.

His travels to the west, exposed him to a society where women enjoyed equal status and contributed equally in the development of their countries. This strengthened his belief that until and unless Indian women were raised to the equal status with men, India could not move ahead.

Though Brahmo Samaj, Arya Samaj, Prathana Samaj and Theosophical Society were actively working for the upliftment of the women, no significant progress was made. Vivekananda was well aware of the activities of all these organizations but was not satisfied with their pace and programme. He resented that all social reform movements were concerned only with the upper class women while poor masses had no place in their schemes. Vivekananda stressed:

"You talk of social reform, but what do you do? All that you mean by your social reforms is either widow-remarriage or female emancipation or something of that sort. Such a scheme may do good to a few no doubt but of what avail is that to a whole nation? Most of you talk social reform of that does not touch the poor masses…"[57]

Though he himself did not initiate or associate with any reform movement yet in his teachings, lectures, conversations and letters, he emphasized the need for upliftment of women in the society.

He declared " All nations have attained greatness, by paying proper respect to women. That country and that nation which do not respect the women have never become great, nor will ever be in future. The principal reason why your race has so much degenerated, is that you had no respect for those living images of Shakti…There is no hope of rise for that family or country where there is no estimation of women, where they live in sadness."[58]

Commenting on Indian men's mentality regarding women, he said:

"We are horrible sinners, and our degradation is due to our calling women 'despicable worms', 'gateway to hell' and so forth. The Lord had said—'Thou art the women, Thou art the man, Thou art the boy and the girl as well'. And we on our part are crying, Be off thou outcast!"[59]

A girl child was considered a burden and the parents used to offer their minor daughter's hand to a middle aged man happily, taking it as their religious duty.

57. J.M. Raisner and N.M. Goldberg ed. *Tilak and the Struggle for Indian Freedom*, PPH, 1966, N.D, p-224.
58. C.W. Vol-VII, p-213.
59. C.W. Vol-VI, 1956, p-224.

Characterizing child marriage as a devilish custom and castigating its supporters Vivekananda said:

"A girl of eight is married to a man of thirty and the parents are jubilant over it....And if anyone protests against it, the plea is put forward, Our religion is being overturned. What sort of religion have they who want to see their girls becoming mothers before they attain puberty even and offer scientific explanations for it."[60]

Though a monk, yet he did not hesitate in criticizing the scriptures and the strictures of local usages, which had reduced the Indian women to lifeless and inert. He repudiated the argument that muslims were responsible for the low state of the hindu women.:

"Many ...lay the blame at the door of the Mohammed an... Just read the Grihya Sutras through and see what is given as the marriageable age of a girl....There is expressly stated that a girl must be married before attaining puberty. The entire Grihya Sutras enjoin this. All the Brahmanas mention them and all the commentators admit them to be true. How can you deny them."[61]

Vivekanand favoured raising the age of marriage of girls. He was in Bombay when the orthodox reaction against the Age of Consent Bill reached its peak. The Bill was a blow to traditional Hindu social arrangements which ensured the subordinate position of the women. He openly attacked the conservative elements who were opposing the Age of Consent Bill, on the ground of being contrary to Hindu religion. He opined:

"The rulers passed the Age of Consent Bill prohibiting a man under the threat of penalty to live with a girl of twelve years, and at once all these so-called leaders of your religion raised a tremendous hue and cry against it, sounding the alarm, 'Alas our religion is lost' As if religion consists in making a girl a mother at the age of twelve or thirteen!"[62]

---

60. C.W. Vol-VI, p-320.
61. Ibid.,
62. C.W. Vol-IV, p-256.

Expressing his anguish, he pointed out:

"Only the other day, when the Age of Consent Bill was being passed, the leaders of the society massed together millions of men to send up their cry, 'we don't want the Bill'. Had this been in any other country, far from getting up meetings to send forth a cry like that, people would have hidden their heads under their roof in shame, that such a calumny could yet stain their society."[63]

He criticised and ridiculed Bharatchandra, a Bengali writer, who was an advocate of child-marriage. He opined that the poems of Bharatchandra should not be taught to the children and 'care should be taken that such books do not come in to the hands of boys.'[64]

During his stay in United States of America, he was amazed to see that women were not dependent upon the menfolk for their survival. They were not dominated by males and enjoyed freedom in every sphere. He wrote letters to his Indian disciples drawing sharp distinctions between the emancipated western women and seclusion of Indian women. He wrote:

"I have never seen women elsewhere as cultured and educated as they are here...Oh, how free they are! It is they who control the social and civic duties, school and colleges are full of women, and in our country women cannot be safely allowed to walk in the streets... Here men treat their women as well as can be desired, and hence they are so prosperous, so learned, so free and so energetic...Few women are married before twenty or twenty-five, and they are as free as the birds in the air. They go to market, school and college earn money and do all kinds of work. Those who are well to do, devote themselves to doing good to the poor. And what are we doing? We are very regular in marrying our girls at eleven years of age lest they should become corrupt and immoral..."[65]

---

63. *Inspired Talks with Swami Vivekananda*, Pub-Advaita Ashram, Almora, 1946, p-58.
64. C.W. Vol-VII, p-225.
65. C.W. Vol-V, p-21-23.

Appreciating the western men's attitude towards women Vivekananda pointed out:

"Westerners are Shakti worshippers in a realistic sense. Woman is given a very great importance. Even in worship it is to Mary that prayers are mostly addressed among the Catholics. 'Ave Maria' is the cry heard everywhere. With the westerners Shakti pooja is not ritualistic as ours but actual. In the West the woman's state is foremost, and great personal attention is paid to her. Such special regard is paid not merely to the noble born or young women, but even to a stranger or a mere acquaintance."[66]

Though women in America enjoyed greater freedom and equality than their counterpart in India yet they too were discriminated and this could not escape the attention of Vivekananda. He regretted that Oxford, Cambridge and Harvard and Yale University were closed for women.

On his return to India, he tried to turn the attention of his countrymen towards the pathetic condition of the Indian women and the need for their upliftmnet.

He planned to set up a Female *Math* and made it known to everyone that girls would be admitted into the proposed Female *Math* only on the condition that their parents agreed to marry them after the age of fifteen.[67] He was the first Hindu saint to recognise Hindu women's right to monastic life, so long enjoyed by the men alone. In the course of a conversation with a disciple, Vivekanand raised the topic of the future *Math* (convent) for women. He said:

"With the Holy Mother as the centre of inspiration, a *Math* is to be established on the eastern bank of the Ganges. As Brahmcharis and Sadhus will be trained in the *Math*, so in other *Math*, Brahmcharinis and Sadhvis will be trained."[68] When his disciple raised objection, the Swami said:

66. C.W. Vol-V, p-408.
67. C.W. Vol-VII, p-213.
68. Modern Review, Jan 1920, p-88.

"It is very difficult to understand why in this country, there is so much difference between men and women whereas Vedanta declares that one conscious self is present in all beings. You always criticise the women but say what you have done for their uplift? Writing Smritis and binding them by hard rules, the men have turned the women into producing machines. If you do not raise the women who are living embodiment of Divine Mother, don't think you have any other way to rise."[69]

The disciple argued against:

"Women are a bondage and a snare to men. Women by their Maya cover the knowledge and dispassion of men. It is for this I suppose that spiritual writers hint that knowledge and devotion is difficult to be attained by them."[70]

Vivekanand replied:

"In what scriptures are such words found that women are not competent for knowledge and divine love? In the period of degradation, when the priests made the other castes incompetent and disentitled to the study of Vedas, they deprived the women of all their rights. Likewise, you find in the Vedic and Upanishadic ages, Maitreyi, Gargi and other women of revered memory, taking the places of Rishis in their knowledge and discussion about Brahman. When such ideal women had commanded of spiritual knowledge, why then shall they not have the same privilege now?"[71]

He stated that in ancient India, the women enjoyed equal rights with men. He told his disciples:

"Again, could anything be more complete than the equality of boys and girls in our old forest universities? Read our Sanskrit dramas—read the story of Shankuntla, and see if Tennyson's 'Princess' has any thing to teach us!"[72]

Again, could anything be more complete than the equality of boys and girls in our old forest universities? Read our Sanskrit dramas— read the story of Shankuntla, and see if Tennyson's 'Princess' has any thing to teach us!

69. C.W. Vol-VII, p-212.
70. Ibid.,
71. Ibid.,
72. C.W. Vol-V, p-161.

He argued in favour of female rights and liberties, the denial which had taken the country backward. Until and unless the people give up narrow outlook and selfish motive for keeping the women enslaved, nation would not progress.

"All narrowness, all contraction, all selfishness is simply slow suicide and when a nation commits the fatal mistake of contracting itself; and of thus cutting of all expansion and life, it must die. Women must go forward or become idiots and soulless tools in the hands of their tyrannical lords. The children are the result of the combination of the tyrant and the idiot and they are slaves."[73]

Indian women were not less capable than their counterparts. He appreciated their feminine modesty, spirit of service, compassion, and contentment. He thought that if the Indian women were given right sort of education, they would well turn out to be the ideal women in the world. He asked them to give up the age-old attitude of helplessness and learn self-defence. He stated:

"They have all the time been trained in helplessness, servile dependence on others, and so they are good only to weep their eyes out at the slightest approach of a mishap or danger. Along with other things they should acquire the spirit of valour and heroism. In the present day it has become necessary for them also to learn self-defence. See how grand was the queen of Jhansi."[74]

If the women were educated, only then would they carry their responsibilities with perfection. "We must see to their growing up as ideal matrons of home in time. The children of such mothers will make further progress in virtues that distinguish the mother. It is only in the homes of educated and pious mothers that great men are born."[75]

They have all the time been trained in helplessness, servile dependence on others, and so they are good only to weep their eyes out at the slightest approach of a mishap or danger. Along with other things they should acquire the spirit of valour and heroism. In the present day it has become necessary for them also to learn self-defence. See how grand was the queen of Jhansi.

73. *Vivekananda Centenary Celebrations*, 1962-63. p-232.
74. C.W. Vol-V, p-258.
75. C.W. Vol-VI, p-489.

In India as well as abroad, Vivekananda never forgot to highlight the intelligence and the virtue of Indian women. In United States, Vivekananda made the Americans know that Indian women were superior to Indian men in intelligence and character. Whenever given an opportunity they outshone the men. In one of his lectures, he quoted John Stuart Mill to prove his viewpoint:

"Women in statesmanship, mananging territories, governing countries, even making war, have proved themselves equal to men...In India I have no doubt of that. Whenever they have had an opportunity they have proved they have as much ability as men, and with this advantage more, that they seldom degenerate; they keep to the moral standard which is innate in their nature, and thus as governors and rulers of their state they prove, at least in India, far superior to men."[76]

So great was his faith in the capability and sincerity of the Indian women that he would say that women could accomplish any task with greater speed than men.

Revive the old arts. Teach your girls fruit-modelling with hardened milk. Give them artistic cooking and sewing. Let them learn painting, photography, the cutting of the designs in paper and gold and silver filigree and embroidery. See that everyone knows something by which she can earn a living, in case of need.

"With five hundred men, he would say, the conquest of India might take fifty years with as many women, not more than a few weeks".[77] He advised his admirers and disciples to provide education to women and make them self-dependent.

"Revive the old arts. Teach your girls fruit-modelling with hardened milk. Give them artistic cooking and sewing. Let them learn painting, photography, the cutting of the designs in paper and gold and silver filigree and embroidery. See that everyone knows something by which she can earn a living, in case of need."[78]

He invited Sister Nivedita, whom he had met in London to come to India and devote herself to the

---

76. Marie Louise Burke *Swami Vivekananda in America-New Discoveries*, Advaita Ashram, Calcutta, 1958, p-415.

77. *The Master As I Saw Him*, Nivedita, p-316.

78. Ibid., p-320.

cause of women education. In a letter written on June 7, 1896, he said:

"Religions of the world have become lifeless mockeries. What the world wants is the character. The world is in need of those whose life is one burning selfless love. That love will make every word tell like thunderbolt...Bold words and bold deeds are what we want."[79]

Explaining about his plan of work, he wrote further:

"I have a definite plan to help the women of my land. I have thought of starting an institution for the education of girls on national lines, producing not only ideal wives or mothers but Brahmcharinis working for the improvement of their own sex. And in this work what is needed is not a man but a woman, a real lioness to work for the Indian women. Your education, sincerity, purity, immense love, determination and above all the Celtic blood make you just the woman wanted."[80]

On the call of Vivekananda, Nivedita decided to dedicate herself to the command of her Master. She came to India and worked till the end of her life.[81] On November 12, 1898, a Girl's School named Nivedita Girls School was started. Along with bookish knowledge, the Swami wanted the girls to be taught vocational courses, so that they could become economically self-dependent. He instructed Nivedita:

"You have no idea of the deliciousness of green mango jam...I am sure you can do this and it could be widening the scope of our work educationally. To be managed entirely by women, think of that! Of course we can make small beginning."[82]

Day after day, he became more emphatic on the need of education for women. Wherever he visited he advocated that the primary education of boys and girls

Religions of the world have become lifeless mockeries. What the world wants is the character. The world is in need of those whose life is one burning love selfless. That love will make every word tell like thunderbolt...Bold words and bold deeds are what we want.

---

81. She came to India at the age of 28 and died in India at the age of 39.
82. Atmaprava, Pravrajika, *Sister Nivedita*, pub, by Sister Nivedita's Girl's School, Calcutta, 1961, p-88.

must be undertaken by women teachers. He regarded this as one excellent means of settling the problem of livlihood for hindu widows. Thus at Sialkot he strongly urged the establishment for an educational institution for girls and as a result of this two day visit, a committee was later formed of the influential men in town, with Lala Mool Chand as Secretary, who at once put the proposal into practice.[83]

He used to exhort all those who used to come to his *Math* for religious lectures and blessings, to work for women.

You all are responsible for this miserable condition of the women and it rests with you also to raise them again. Therefore I say, set to work. What will it do to memorize a few religious books like the Vedas and so on.

"You all are responsible for this miserable condition of the women and it rests with you also to raise them again. Therefore I say, set to work. What will it do to memorize a few religious books like the Vedas and so on."[84]

However, in his opinion, the women had to play a major role in their own salvation and for this he wanted them to be equipped with the power of knowledge, to be self-dependent by learning various arts.

He also suggested, women go to foreign countries and see for themselves how women were contributing in the development of their countries. He wanted women emancipation and empowerment but did not want the Indian women to imitate the western women blindly. He wanted them to grow on the national lines, to follow their own culture. Indian women should follow Sita, Savitri, Chand Sultana, the queen of Golconda and Laxmi Bai, the queen of Jhansi as their role model and should be dedicated wives and mothers as well. He assigned women a greater role in the regeneration of India and wanted them to work along with men in building a new India.

Thus in the social context Vivekananda was mainly concerned with the plight of the Shudras and the enslavement of the women, the two together formed

---

83. *Vivekananda in Indian Newspapers*, p-582, 606.
84. C.W. Vol-VII, p-216.

about eighty per cent of the total hindu population. He categorically blamed the Brahmins particularly the priests for inventing, maintaining and consolidating the caste system, thereby maintaining their own hegemony on the social heirarchy—grabbing all the privileges, depriving women of all rights, placing them under male-domination, designating a large number of hindus as shudras and degrading them to the state of animals. He sought abolition of such priestly class in the new social set up.

He emphasized the need for education which would enable people for finding solutions and work towards the desired reforms. However, he also knew that without political and economic empowerment of the socially under-privileged sections including women, social equality would not be possible. Hence, he wanted equal share for them in the governance of the future independent India—to ensure justice to all and save it from disintegration.

3
Chapter

An Iconoclastic Ascetic

"Heavens, hells and incarnations—all nonsense !"

— Swami Vivekananda

Vivekananda was for rational approach even in the matter of religion. He used to say "if a religion is destroyed by rational investigation, it was not a religion at all but a superstition...All that was dross, would be taken away and the essential parts would emerge triumphant from such investigation".[1]

His ideas on religion are revolutionary and seem to come from the mouth of an athiest rather than a monk.

"Science and religion are both attempts to help us out of the bondage; only religion is more ancient, and we have the superstition that it is more holy."[2]

Referring to science and scientific discussions, he explained:

"What is meant by science is, that explanations of things are in their own nature, and that no external being or existence are required to explain what is going on in the universe. The chemist never requires demons or ghosts, or any thing of that sort, to explain his phenomena. The physicist never requires any one of these to explain the things he knows. Nor does any other scientist. And this is one of the features of science that I want to apply to religion. In this, religions are found wanting and that is why they are crumbling into pieces. Every science wants its explanation from inside,

> Science and religion are both attempts to help us out of the bondage; only religion is more ancient, and we have the superstition that it is more holy.

1. Swami Chetnanda, *Vedanta-voice of Freedom*, Advaita Ashram Calcutta, 1991. p-94.
2. C.W. Vol-VII, 1947, p-103.

from the very nature of things; and religions are not able to supply this."[3] According to him it is useless to look into *shastras*, or stars for the explanation of any phenomenon.

"If you can get an explanation of a phenomenon from within its nature, it is nonsense to look for an explanation from outside. Have you found any phenomena in the life of a man that you have ever seen which cannot be explained by the power of man himself? So what is the use of going to the stars or anything else in the world."[4]

Vivekananda was against believing anything—even religion and God—without reasoning and self experience. He wanted to see God with his own eyes. While he was still a child, this quest took him at midnight to the banana groove to find Hanuman the monkey God. He stayed there for hours but was disappointed. When he grew up he went to Dabendranath Tagore, Swami Ramakrishna and later Pavhari Baba for the same. He visited Bodh Gaya and meditated under the Bodhi tree to get revelation like Buddha. He contented with Ramakrishna about Radhakrishna episode. He doubted the historicity of the tale and considered the relationship of Lord Krishna with Radha immoral and objectionable.[5] He would tell his Master, "I am God. You are God, these created things are God—what can be more absurd than this. The sage who wrote such things must have been insane."[6]

He doubted the existence of God even after becoming a monk. His gurubhai writes that in Baranagore monastery, Vivekananda would discuss theories of Kant, Hegel, Mill and Spencer...If the talk was whether God existed or not, Naren would prove

---

Sidebar: If you can get an explanation of a phenomenon from within its nature, it is nonsense to look for an explanation from outside. Have you found any phenomena in the life of a man that you have ever seen which cannot be explained by the power of man himself? So what is the use of going to the stars or anything else in the world.

Sidebar: He would tell his Master, "I am God. You are God, these created things are God-what can be more absured than this. The sage who wrote such things must have been insane.

---

3. C.W. Vol-I 1947, p-373.
4. C.W. Vol-IV 1948, p-184.
5. *Life*, Vol-I 1979, p-17, 94.
6. Ibid., p-96.

with the backing of logic and reason that God was a myth."[7]

It seems that Swami Ramakrishna could not show him God for which Naren had become his disciple. He was disappointed. He told his fellow monks:

"I am dissatisfied with everything, even talking to devotees has become distasteful to me. It seems that there is no such thing as God."[8]

His non-belief in the existence of God amazed everyone. He was a monk but sought proof of the existence of God. While in United States, he boldly expressed his views before the believers:

"How can we understand that Moses saw God unless we too see Him? If God ever came to anyone He will come to me. I will go to God direct; let Him talk to me. I cannot take belief as a basis that is atheism and blasphamy. If God spoke to a man in the desert of Arabia two thousand years ago, He can also speak to him today, else how can I know that He has not died?"[9]

Like a scientist he believed in the law of evolution i.e., everything comes up from the lower kingdom. He refuted the theories given in the *shastras* that man and the entire universe was the creation of God. In his numerous statements he explained that man is the creator of God and not God the creator of man. His iconoclastic ideas caused a stir wherever he spoke. The orthodox cursed him and the common people unaccustomed to such preaching were astonished.

"Down with superstitions! Neither scriptures nor gods exist. Down with temples, with priests, with gods, with incarnations, with God hiself!..Truth alone triumphs, and this is true. I am the infinite...Time is in me, not I in time. God was born in mind. God the Father, Father of the universe...he is created by me in my own mind."[10]

---

7. Ibid., p-163.
8. Ibid., p-202.
9. C.W. Vol-VII, 1947, p-93.
10. C.W. Vol-I, p-502.

He used to boldly say that the highest God is man in the entire universe.

"There is no God separate form you, no God higher than you, the real 'you.'

All the Gods are little beings to you, all the ideas of the soul and Father in the heaven are but your reflection. God himself is your image...Throughout the universe we are creating gods after our own image.[11]

We are the greatest God that ever was or will be...bow down to nothing but to your own higher self. Your own will is that answer prayers.[12]

What can prevail over you? You are the God of the universe. Where can you seek for help. Never help came from anywhere but from yourself. In your ignorance every prayer that you made and that was answered, you thought was answered by some Being, but you answered the prayer yourself unknowingly. The help came from yourself and you fondly imagined that someone was sending help to you. There is no help for you outside of yourself; you are the creator of this universe.[13]

Man is higher than all animals, than all angels; none is greater than man. Even the Devas (God) will have to come down again and again to perfection through a human body. Man alone attains to perfection, not even the Devas.[14]

We can have no conception of God higher than man, so our God is man and man is God.[15]

It was radical to say that God is in us and it is futile to find him outside of ourselves and hence man should believe in himself.

"Believe first in yourself than in God. A handful of strongmen will move the world...One man contains

> We are the greatest God that ever was or will be...bow down to nothing but to your own higher self. Your own will is that answer prayers.

> Believe first in yourself than in God. A handful of strongmen will move the world...One man contains within him the whole universe. One particle of matter has all the energy of the universe at its back.

---

11. C.W. Vol-III, p-24.
12. C.W. Vol-VII, p-76.
13. C.W. Vol-III, 1948, p-26.
14. C.W. Vol-I, p-142.
15. C.W. Vol-III, p-28.

within him the whole universe. One particle of matter has all the energy of the universe at its back."[16]

He struck at the very root of dogmatic and theological belief in a personal God in heaven.

"What is the idea of God in heaven? ...God sitting up on a cloud. Think of the utter blasphemy of it....These masses of foolish beliefs and superstitions hinder our progress."[17]

According to him heaven is mere superstition. Heaven or hell does not exist anywhere except on this earth.

"This one life is the universal life, heavens and all those places are here. All the Gods are here, the prototypes of man. ..We have been projecting our little doubles, and we are the originals of these gods, we are the real, the only gods to be worshipped."[18]

He declared in America, "God is not a king sitting away in one corner of the universe to deal out punishment or rewards according to man's deeds here on earth.[19]

Reason and rationale should be the yardstick to measure everything including religion.[20]

"Why was reason given to us if we have to believe? It is not tremendously blasphemous to believe against reason? What rights have we not to use the greatest gift that God has given to us? I am sure that God will pardon a man who will use his reason and cannot believe, rather than a man who believes blindly instead of using his faculties He has given him. He simply degrade his nature and goes down to the level of the beast-degrades his senses and dies."[21]

> This one life is the universal life, heavens and all those places are here. All the Gods are here, the prototypes of man. ..We have been projecting our little doubles, and we are the originals of these gods, we are the real, the only gods to be worshipped.

> Why was reason given to us if we have to believe? It is not tremendously blasphemous to believe against reason? What rights have we not to use the greatest gift that God has given to us?

16. Santi L. Mukherjee, *The Philosophy of Man-Making*, New Oriental Book Agency, Calcutta, 1971, p-133.
17. C.W. Vol-VIII, p-126-27.
18. C.W. Vol-II, p-325, Rept-1968.
19. Marie Louise Burke, *Swami Vivekananda in America-New Discoveries*, Advaita Ashram, Calcutta, 1958, p-154.
20. C.W. Vol-II, 1970, p-321.
21. C.W. Vol-VI, p-12, 1956.

Emphasising the application of reason in religion, Vivekananda made it clear that the first test of the true teaching must be that teaching should not contradict reason.

"There must be some independent authority and that cannot be any book but something which is universal; and what is more universal than reason.? It has been said that reason is not strong enough; it does not always help us to get at the truth; many a times it makes mistake and therefore, the conclusion is that we must believe in the authority of the church...On the other hand I should say, if reason be so weak, a body of priests would be weaker, and I am not going to accept their verdict but I will abide by my reason because with all its weakness there is some chance of my getting at the truth through it; while by the other means, there is no such hope at all."[22]

At another place speaking on the same theme Vivekananda declared:

"Everything religion claims must be judged from the standpoint of reason. Why religion should claim that they do not abide by the standpoint of reason...If one does not apply the standard of reason, there cannot be any true judgement even in the case of religions."[23]

Commenting on the uncritical approach of the Hindus, Vivekananda wrote in a letter to Pandit Shankarlal on 20th September 1892, as:

"The Hindu mind is ever deductive and never synthetic or inductive. In all our philosophies, we always find hair-splitting arguments, taking for granted some general proposition, but the proposition itself may be as childish as possible. Nobody ever asked or searched the truth of these general propositions. Therefore, independent thought we have almost none to speak of, and hence the death of those sciences which are the results of observation and generalization."[24]

Everything religion claims must be judged from the standpoint of reason. Why religion should claim that they are not abide by the standpoint of reason...If one does not apply the standard of reason, there cannot be any true judgement even in the case of religions.

22. C.W. Vol-II, p-335-36. Rept-1968.
23. Ibid., p-335.
24. *Letters of Swami Vivekananda*, Prabudha Bharta, 1950, p-54.

He regarded scientific knowledge not less important than religion.

"In our country we go down on our knees before the man who reads *vedas*, and we do not care for the man who is studying physics. That is superstition."[25]

"Avoid everyone, however great and good he may be, who asks you to believe blindly. It is healthier for the individual or the race to remain wicked than to be made apparently good by such morbid extraneous control"[26]

At another place he said:

It is better that mankind should become atheist through following reason than blindly believe in two hundred million gods on the authority of anybody.[27]

"There is some hope for the atheists because though they differ from others, they think for themselves. The people who never think anything for themselves are not yet born into the world of religion; they have a mere jelly-fish existence."[28]

In a letter written to his disciple in 1894 he remarked:

"Do not believe in what you have heard", says the great Buddha, "do not believe in doctrines because they have been handed down to you through generations; do not believe in anything because it is followed blindly by many; do not believe because some old sage makes a statement; do not believe in truths to which you have become attached by habit; do not believe merely on the authority of your teachers and elders. Have deliberation and analyse, and when the result agrees with reason and conduces to the good of one and all, accept it and live up to it."[29]

Speaking about himself, Vivekananda said:

"I believe in reason and follow reason, having seen enough of the evils of authority."[30]

In our country we go down on our knees before the man who reads *vedas*, and we do not care for the man who is studying physics. That is superstition.

It is better that mankind should become atheist through following reason than blindly believe in two hundred million gods on the authority of anybody.

I believe in reason and follow reason, having seen enough of the evils of authority.

25. C.W. Vol-VIII, p-137, 1951. Rept-1959.
26. Ibid., p-165.
27. *Lectures from Colombo to Almora*, p-199.
28. C.W. Vol-IV, p-123, 1947.
29. Ibid., p-217.
30. C.W. Vol-II, p-336, 1968.

"I believe in thinking independently. I believe in becoming entirely free from the holy teachers; pay all reverence to them, but look at religion as an independent research. I have to find my light, just as they found theirs."[31]

"We must reason; and when reason prove to us the truth of these Prophets and great men about whom the ancient books speak in every country, we shall believe them."[32]

He appealed to the people not to believe in superstitions, the sign of degradation and death:

"Mystery-mongering and superstition are always sign of death. Therefore, beware of them; be strong and stand on your feet....Do not run after these superstitions. Better for you and for the race that you become rank atheist, because you would have strength...Shame on humanity that strong men should spend their time on these superstitions, spend all their time in inventing allergies to explain the most rotten superstitions of the world. Be bold; do not try to explain everything that way."[33]

He did not believe in miracles and regarded them as stumbling blocks in the path of truth. He characterized the performer of miracles as 'clever jugglers' and their miracles as 'tricks'.[34]

"Chasing after physical illusion was wastage of energy of mind and had nothing to do with the realities of the life.

...better die as unbeliever than be played upon as cheats and jugglers. The power of reasoning was given to you for use.[35]

All this false love of mystery should be knocked on the head, the first time it comes into your mind.[36]

31. Ibid., p-45.
32. C.W. Vol-VI, 1956, p-12.
33. C.W. Vol-III, 1948, p-279.
34. Marie Louise, Burke, p-515.
35. C.W. Vol-IV, 1948, p-57.
36. Ibid., p-56.

He asked the people not to believe in those religions which promote superstitions and irrational practices as occultism. He explained:

"Religions have immense capacity to raise false issues; instead of promoting spirituality they often talk of spiritualism and occultism and they may also promote obscurantism and illogic. But religion that integrates the head with the heart can meet science and even spur science."[37]

He considered it a complete contradiction to Indian tradition, to make religious truth the monopoly of a handful of people hidden away somewhere.

"It was never preached on this soil that the truths of religion are 'mysteries' that they are the property of secret societies sitting on the snow-caps of the Himalayas...I have been in the Himalayas. I am a sanyasi. For fourteen years I have been on my feet. These mysterious societies do not exist anywhere. Don't run after superstitions!"[38]

"We have become weak and that is why occultism and mysticism come to us, these creepy things...have nearly destroyed us."[39]

> We have become weak and that is why occultism and mysticism come to us, these creepy things...have nearly destroyed us.

Theosophical Society in his opinion was causing a lot of harm to the Indian society by promoting occultism. He declared that its 'occultism and esotericism' would make Indians, who were already weak and superstitious, weaker and more superstitious. 'Give up these weakening mysticism' and part from all these mysterious things all these weakening things."[40] He assailed the Theosophists for making an attempt to give a rational explanation, to forms and observances apparently unmeaning to most people but being practised by them nevertheless.[41]

---

37. Swami Swahananda, *Service and Spirituality*, Ramakrishna Math, Madras 1979, p-60.
38. *Lectures from Colombo to Almora*, p-137 & C.W. III, p-224.
39. Ibid. p-137.
40. Amiya Sen, *Hindu Revivalism in Bengal*, Oxford University Press. N.D. 1993, p-295.
41. *Vivekananda in Indian Newspapers*, p-166.

Vivekananda told his disciples and admirers about his disbelief in occults as:

"I do not believe in the occult. If a thing be unreal it is not. What is unreal does not exist. Strange things are natural phenomenon. I know them to be matter of science. I do not believe in occult societies. They do no good and can never do good."[42]

To a credulous gentleman who believed in occults, superstition etc., and insisted upon the supernatural powers, Vivekananda said "It is this nonsense, which is demoralizing our nation.[43]

It is a disease, a morbid desire. It degenerates the race, weakens the nerves and the brain. Living in incessant morbid fear of hobgoblins or stimulating the hunger for wonders; all these wild stories about them keep the nerves at an unnatural tension-a slow and sure degeneration of the race."[44]

At Srinagar he rebuked a man practicing palmistry and asked his admirers not to believe in astrology, as it too was the sign of a weak mind. He said:

"You will find that astrology and all these mystical things are generally signs of weak mind; therefore as soon as they are becoming prominent in our minds, we should see a physician, take good food and rest."[45]

To enlightened the people he used to narrate the following story:

"There is an old story of an astrologer who came to a king and said 'You are going to die in six months'. The king was frightened out of his wits and was almost about to die then and there out of fear. But his minister was a clever man, and this man told the king that these astrologers were fools. The king would not believe him. So the minister saw no other way to make the king see that they were fools but to invite the astrologer to the

You will find that astrology and all these mystical things are generally signs of weak mind; therefore as soon as they are becoming prominent in our minds, we should see a physician, take good food and rest.

42. Ibid., p-81.
43. *Life*, Vol-I, p-213.
44. C.W. Vol-IV, 1948, p-58.
45. C.W. Vol-VIII, 1959, p-184. (Reprint 1977).

palace again. Then he asked him if his calculations were correct. The astrologer said that there could not be a mistake, but to satisfy him he went through the whole of the calculation again and said that they were perfectly correct. The king's face became livid. The minister said to the astrologer, 'And when do you think you will die?' 'In twelve years', was the reply. The minister quickly drew his sword and separated the astrologer's head from his body and said to the king, 'Do you see the liar? He is dead this moment."[46]

He refuted the concept that man is commanded by God and all his actions are pre-determined. He regarded man the maker of his own destiny.

"We human beings are very slow to recognize our own weakness, our own faults, so long as we can lay all the blame upon somebody else. Men in general lay all blame of life on their fellow men, or failing that on God, or they conjure up a ghost, and say it is fate. Where is fate, and who is fate? We reap what we sow. We are the makers of our own fate."[47]

'It is coward and the fool who says, 'This is fate'. But it is the strong man who stands up and say, 'I will make my fate.'[48]

He advised people not to bear oppression on the ground that it was due to their past *karma* (deeds) but to retaliate and revolt against the oppressor. Sister Nivedita writes:

"....at Almora, I remember a certain elderly man with a face full of amiable weakness, who came to put to him, a question about *Karma*. What were they to do, he asked whose *Karma* it was to see the strong oppress the weak?. The swami turned on him in surprised indignation. 'Why thrash the strong, of course!'. He said further, 'You forget your own part in this Karma—Yours is always the right to rebel!"[49]

---

46. Ibid.,
47. C.W. Vol-II, 1970, p-224.
48. C.W. Vol-VIII, Reprint 1977, p-184.
49. Nivedita, *The Master As I Saw Him*, p-118.

He asked the religious leaders to give up preaching the theory of *Karma* which makes man helpless and inactive and therby cause harm to the country as well. To a preacher of the cow-protection society who had refused to help the famine-stricken people on the ground that their state was due to their *karma*, Vivekananda shouted:

"If you make a plea of *Karma*, then it becomes a settled fact that it is useless to try on struggle for every thing in the world and your work for the protection of cow is no exception. With regards to your case also, it can be said, the mother cow through their own *Karma* falls into the hands of the butchers and we need not do anything in the matter,"[50]

He challenged the theory that great men and their personages were divinely ordained:

"All knowledge is possessed exclusively by some extraordinary great men and those special personages take birth by the command of the God, or in conformity to a higher law of nature, or in some preordained order of Karma; except through the agency of these great ones, there is no other way of attaining knowledge. If such a view be correct and certain, there seems to be no necessity for any individual to strive hard to find any new and original truth—all originality is lost to society for want of exercise and encouragement; and the worst of all is that, society tries to oppose and stop any attempt in the original direction and thus the faculty of the initiative dies out. If it is finally settled that the path of human welfare is for ever chalked out by these omniscient men, society naturally fears its own destruction if the least deviation be made from the boundary line of the path, and so it tries to compel all men through rigid laws and threats of punishment to follow that path with unconditional obedience. If society succeeds in imposing such obedience to itself by confining all men within the narrow groove of these paths, then the destiny of mankind becomes no better

---

50. C.W. Vol-VI, 1956, p-450-51.

than that of machine. If every act in man's life has been all previously determined, then what need is there for the culture of the faculty of thought—where is the field for the free play of independent thought and action? In course of time, for want of proper use all activity is given up, all originality is lost, a sort of Tamasika (darkness) dreamy lifelessness hovers over the whole nation, and headlong it goes down and down. The death of such a nation is not far to seek."[51]

He was scornful of fraudulent Sadhus. During his travels in northern India with his foreign disciples, he came across a large number of Sadhus. Vivekananda found that their religosity was a pretention and not genuine. Explaining the reason of their large numbers, Vivekananda said: "... the number of *Sadhus* is a legion here; but speaking of them as a class morally and spiritually they are very much degenerated. Many jats and agriculturists in these provinces unable to earn their living by the sweat of their brow became *Sadhus* and it is these men whose teaching instead of making people religious, is decidedly doing them harm."[52]

He urged the people to wake up as ignorance, pretentions and deception were taking the country downwards. The dross that had covered the real spirituality had to be wiped off in order to take the country forward.

"Do you not see—taking up the plea of Sattava, the country has been slowly and slowly drowned in the Ocean of Tamas or dark ignorance? Where the most dull, want to hide their stupidity by covering with a false desire for the Highest Knowledge, which is beyond all activities and bred in life-long laziness, want to throw the veil of renunciation and over his own unfitness for the work; where the most diabolical try to make their cruelty appear under the cloak of austerity, as a part of religion; where no one has an eye upon his own incapacity, but everyone is ready to lay the whole blame

---

51. *Swami Vivekananda in Indian Newspapers,* p-63.
52. C.W. Vol-IV, p-338, 1948.

on others; where knowledge consists only in getting in some books by heart, genius consists in chewing the cud of others thoughts, and the highest glory consists in taking the name of ancestors; do we require any other proof to show that country is being drowned in utter Tamas?"[53] The practitioners of religious ceremonies according to him were wretches who were to be blamed for the slackness which had engulfed the entire nation.

"Those whose heads have a tendency to be troubled day and night over such questions as whether the bell should ring on the right or on the left, whether the sandal-paste mark should be on the head or anywhere else, whether the light should be waved twice or four times—simply deserve the name of wretches, and it is owing to that sort of notion that we are the outcasts of Fortune, kicked and spurned at, while the people of the West are the masters of the whole world..."[54]

Exhorting the people to beware of such practitioners and to stop wasting time in discussing nonsensical issues, he said:

"Give up all those discussions, old fights about things which are meaningless, which are nonsensical in their very nature. Think of the last 600 or 700 years of degradation, when grown-up men by hundreds have been discussing for years, whether we should drink a glass of water with the right hand or the left, whether the hand should be washed three times or four times, whether five times we should gurgle or six times. What can you expect from men who pass their lives in discussing such momentous questions as these and writing most learned philosophies on these questions."[55]

He regretted that hindus blindly follow anything in the name of religion and were not prepared for the new rationalistic interpretations.

"Any number of lies in the name of religious book are all right. In India if I want to teach anything new, and

> Those whose heads have a tendency to be troubled day and night over such questions as whether the bell should ring on the right or on the left, whether the sandal-paste mark should be on the head or anywhere else, whether the light should be waved twice or four times—simply deserve the name of wretches, and it is owing to that sort of notion that we are the outcasts of Fortune, kicked and spurned at, while the people of the West are the masters of the whole world...

---

53. C.W. Vol-VI, 1956, p-264.
54. C.W. Vol-III, 1948 p-270.
55. C.W, Vol-IV, 1948, p-41.

simply state it on my own authority; as what I think, nobody will come to listen to me; but if I take some passage from the Vedas and juggle with it and give it to the most impossible meaning, murder everything that is reasonable in it and bring out my own ideas as the ideas that were meant by the Vedas, all the fools will follow me in the crowd."[56]

Vivekananda asked the people to be independent of religious authorities and to form independent judgements:

"...lying complacently on the bed and ringing the bell now and then is a sort of disease, pure and simple. Be independent, learn to form independent judgements. That such and such a chapter of such and such Tantra has prescribed a standard length for the handle of a bell—what matters it to me? Through the Lords will out of our lips shall come millions of Vedas and Tantras and Puranas."[57]

Religious truths cannot be confined to a particular book or prophet. These are universal and one who follows them in real life is the truly religious man.

"If religion and life depend upon books or upon the existence of any Prophet whatsoever, then perish all religions and books. Religion is in us."[58]

According to him as long as religion was in the hands of a chosen few, or of a body of priests, it will be in temples, churches, books, dogmas, ceremonials, forms and rituals only. But it is not the real religion.[59]

'Religion is not going to Church or putting marks on the forehead, or dressing in a particular fashion; you may paint yourselves in all the colours of the rainbow, but if the heart has not been opened, if you have not realized God, it is all in vain.'[60]

...lying complacently on the bed and ringing the bell now and then is a sort of disease, pure and simple. Be independent, learn to form independent judgements. That such and such a chapter of such and such Tantra has prescribed a standard length for the handle of a bell—what matters it to me? Through the Lords will out of our lips shall come millions of Vedas and Tantras and Puranas.

Religion is not going to Church or putting marks on the forehead, or dressing in a particular fashion; you may paint yourselves in all the colours of the rainbow, but if the heart has not been opened, if you have not realized God, it is all in vain.

---

56. C.W. Vol-VI 1956, p-265.
57. C.W. Vol-VII, 1947, p-83.
58. C.W. Vol-III, 1948, p-283.
59. C.W. Vol-II, 1968, p-68.
60. C.W. Vol-III, 1948, p-283.

'Going to temple becomes tantamount to spiritual life. Giving something to priest becomes tantamount to religious life. These are dangerous and pernicious and should be at once checked.'[61]

He bitterly criticized the priests for their selfishness and regarded them responsible for the wide discrepancy between the liberal doctrine of *advaita,* preaching universal brotherhood and its perverse application by them. According to him:

"Through selfishness they introduced a large number of strange, non-Vedic, immoral and unreasonable doctrines—simply to keep intact their own prestige and it was the Brahmin who made a monopoly of the religious books and kept the question of sanction and prohibition in their own hands...if you can but spend enough money, the priest class is ready to write out whatever sanctions or prohibitions you want!"[62]

Bengal in 1897 was in the grip of a famine and millions of Bengalis were dying of hunger. However, the priest were unconcerned and continued charging for their religious services. The Swami could not bear this and lamented, "In India there is famine now, but there are temples in each one of which are jewels worth a king's ransom! If the priest taught this impersonal idea to the people, their occupation would be gone.[63]

Priestcraft and tyranny go hand in hand. Why was it invented?

Because some strong men in old times got people into their hands and said, you must obey us or we will destroy you. ..It is the idea of thunderer who kills everyone who does not obey him.[64]

The priests only give us an assurance that if we follow them, listen to their admonitions, and walk in the way they have marked for us—then when we die, they will give us a passport to enable us to see the face of God!

61. C.W. Vol-II, 1968, p-320.
62. Ibid.,
63. C.W. III, 1948, p-414.
64. C.W. II, 1968, p-30.

What are all these heaven ideas but simply modification of this nonsensical priestcraft?[65]

Priestcraft is the bane of India...Priestcraft is in its nature cruel and heartless. That is why religion goes down where Priestcraft arises. Says the Vedanta, We must give up the idea of privilege, then will religion come, be men, kick out the priests who are always against progress, because they would never mend, their hearts would never become big. They are the offspring of centuries of superstition and tyranny. Root out priest class first.[66]

Challenging the supremacy of the Brahmins, he stated that the Kshtriyas' contribution to hinduism was greater than them. He regarded Kshtriyas the fathers of all that is noble and beautiful in hinduism. "Who wrote the Upanishads? Who was Rama? Who was Krishna? Who was Buddha? Who were the Tirthankaras of the Jains? Whenever the Kshtriyas have preached religion, they have given it to everybody; and whenever the Brahmins wrote anything, they would deny all rights to others. Read the Gita and the Sutras of Vyasa, or get someone to read them to you. In the Gita the way is laid open to all men and women, to all caste and colour, but Vyasa tries to put meanings upon the Vedas to cheat the poor Shudras. Is God a nervous fool like you that the flow of His river of mercy would be dammed up by a piece of meat? If such be He, His value is not a pie!"[67]

He was critical of some of the holy scriptures of hinduism, characterizing the writers of Samritis and Puranas as men of limited intelligence, Vivekananda wrote to his disciple Pramada Das Mitra on 30th May, 1897:

"The Samritis and Puranas are productions of men of limited intelligence and are full of fallacies, errors, the feelings of class and malice. Only parts of them

> The Samritis and Puranas are productions of men of limited intelligence and are full of fallacies, errors, the feelings of class and malice. Only parts of them breathing broadness of spirit and love are acceptable, the rest is to be rejected.

---

65. C.W. Vol-V, 1947, p-8.
66. C.W. Vol-IV 1948, p-305.
67. Ibid.,

breathing broadness of spirit and love are acceptable, the rest is to be rejected."[68]

He suggested that only those portions of the Vedas should be accepted which agree with reason.[69]

Contrary to Vivekananda, Swami Dayananda regarded Vedas absolutely free from error and an authority unto themselves.

Vivekananda's critical study of Ramayana found Ravana a civilised king and the civilization of Lanka higher than that of Ayodhya. In his lecture on East and West, he boldly placed his view-point.

Vivekananda resented and opposed the religious leaders' intervention in social affairs. "What business had the priests to interfere in every social matter.?[70]

You must bear in mind that religion has to do only with the soul and has no business to interfere in social matters.[71]

In a letter to his disciple, Mrinalini Bose, Vivekananda wrote:

"Rishi Muni or God—none has the power to force an institution on the society. When the needs of the times press hard on it, society adopts certain customs for self-preservation, Rishis have only recorded those customs.[72]

Social laws were created by economic conditions under the sanction of the religion. The terrible mistake of religion was to interfere in the social matters...we insist at the same time that religion has no right to become a law giver. Hands off! Keep yourself to your own bounds and everything would come right."[73]

> You must bear in mind that religion has to do only with the soul and has no business to interfere in social matters.

---

68. *Letters*, p-383.
69. C.W. Vol-VIII, 1959, p-20.
70. C.W. Vol-IV, 1948, p-304.
71. Ibid.,
72. Letters, p-422.
73. Ibid., p-90.

He explained that social customs were the product of the local enviornment and that is why they vary from region to region.

"The Brahmins of Southern India...would shrink in horror at the sight of another Brahmin eating meat; a Brahmin in the North thinks it a glorious and holy thing to do—he kills goat by the hundred in sacrifice. ....The greatest mistake made is that ignorant people always think that this local custom is the sense of our religion."[74]

He never made secret of his views. Quoting verses from *Uttara Ramchritra,* he boldly stated that in ancient times brahmins used to take meat and even beef and were called upon to kill cows and other animals for Yajna. In Madura on 3 February 1897, Vivekananda stated before a gathering of 2000 people that in ancient India, Aryans partook cow's flesh and it was prohibited because of economic and not religious reasons. Eating or not eating beef was not linked with religion. It was a non-essential part of the religion, which existed in ancient India but was discontinued afterwards. He stated in his lecture on Buddhist India, "You will be astonished if I tell you, that according to the old ceremonials, he is not a good Hindu who does not eat beef."[75]

In the first edition of the *Satyartha Prakash,* published in 1874 even Swami Dayananda approved of beef eating but in the second edition it is condemned.[76]

Non-observance or changing the customs and practices were in the domain of the social matters and hence had been changed in the past as well.

"This you have always to remember that because a little social custom is going to be changed, you are not going to lose your religion at all. Remember these customs have already been changed. There was a time

74. *Lectures from Colombo to Almora,* p-79.
75. C.W. III, 1948, p-536. Also see *Life* Vol-I, p-308, 335.
76. In 1882 he founded a Gorakshani Sabha (Cow-Protection Society) J.N. Farquhar, *Modern Religious Movements* in India, Munshiram, Manoharlal, N.D, 1967, p-111.

in this very India when, without eating beef, no Brahmin could remain a Brahmin; you read in the Vedas, how a Sanyasin, a king or a great man came into a house, the best bullock was killed; how in time it was found that we were an agricultural race, killing the best bulls meant annihilation of the race. Therefore the practice was stopped, and a voice was raised against the killing of cows. Sometimes we find existing then what we now consider the most horrible custom. In course of time other laws had to be made."[77]

Citing from Shastras, the Swami stated that in ancient India, it was a common practice to sacrifice animals on certain occasions, such as Shraddha and if one omitted to kill animals at that time, he was considered a sinner. He quoted Manu, saying that "if those who were invited to the ceremonies did not partake of the animal food offered there, they had to take birth in an animal body in their next life."[78] He also pointed out that instances were there in Ramayana and the Mahabharta of drinking of wine and the taking of meat by God Rama and Krishna.[79]

When asked about what he considered the most glorious period of the Indian history, Vivekananda answered that 'it was the vedic period when five brahmins used to polish off one cow.'[80]

Thus killing cow and eating beef was not irreligiousness. Even Swami Ramakrishna was not against it. When he practised Islam, he too used to eat Muslim food. Vivekananda's biographers write how once when Vivekananda told his master that he had taken what was considered forbidden food, the latter said: 'That will not affect you in the least. If one can keep one's mind steadily on God, eating beef or pork…"[81]

---

77. *Lectures from Colombo to Almora*, p-80.
78. Ibid., p-82.
79. Ibid.,
80. S. Sarma, *The Renaissance of Hinduism,* Benares Hindu University, 1944, p-96.
81. *Life*. Vol-I, p-93, 1979.

The orthodox Brahmins never forgave Vivekananda's ideologies. Undaunted Vivekananda stuck to his understanding of the religion and advocated animal food for hindus, if they were to cope at all with the rest of the world.

"The real fact however is that the nations who take animal food are, as a rule brave, heroic and most thoughtful....when the Hindus used to make Yajnas with animal sacrifices in India and used to take the meat of the animals sacrificed, then only great genius were born among them; but since the taking of the Hindus to Babaji's vegetarianism not one great man arose from amidst them.[82]

...forcing of vegetarianism upon those who have to earn their bread by labouring day and night, is one of the causes of the loss of our national freedom."[83]

Non-violence preached by Emperor Ashoka, according to Vivekananda caused tremendous harm to the country and ultimately led to its enslavement. In one of his lectures given after his return from west, Vivekananda argued:

"It is true that Emperor Ashoka saved the lives of millions of animals by the threat of the sword; but is not the slavery of thousand years more dreadful than that."[84]

In his opinion non-vegetarian diet was good for health for the nation as well. In an article entitled 'The East and the West' the Swami wrote: "Whatever one or the other say, the real fact, however, is, that the nations who take animal food are always, as a rule, notably brave, heroic and thoughtful."[85]

Swami Dayananda preached against non-vegetarianism as it involves the infliction of pain and slaughter of other living beings. Giving a scientific explanation to the issue Vivekananda said:

82. C.W. Vol-V, 1947, p-385.
83. Ibid., p-386.
84. C.W. Vol-IV, p-486.
85. C.W. Vol-V, p-385.

It is impossible to sustain life without killing some other forms of life. Vegetations too are living being and their destruction is also killing.

It is impossible to sustain life without killing some other forms of life. Vegetations too are living being and their destruction is also killing.

Most of these rules and prohibitions about food must have arisen from consideration of health and local conditions…In modern times most of these taboos have been abandoned."[86]

He countered all the arguments against meat-eating put forward by Swami Dayananda.

"Some say animal food produces so many diseases. As against this, it is pointed out that if this is true, non-vegetarian races like the English, American etc., must have been the most unhealthy and the Hindus most healthy people. But this is not so in fact. Next it is contended that those who eat goats and swine will have the brain like the brains of those animals. To this it may be replied that on this principle, potato and brinjal eaters must have potato and brinjal brains. It is argued that all chemicals of the animal food are contained in vegetable food also, and the former is therefore superfluous. As against this, it can be replied that the elements of these chemicals are all there in water and sunlight. Why not subsist on them only.[87]

It is seen that nations that live on animal food are found on the whole, stronger, more courageous and warlike. They have overcome the vegetarian races and dominated over them. So the conclusion is that in a world where there is struggle for existence, nations and races have to take animal food, if they are not to be overcome and enslaved by others.

It is seen that nations that live on animal food are found on the whole, stronger, more courageous and warlike. They have overcome the vegetarian races and dominated over them. So the conclusion is that in a world where there is struggle for existence, nations and races have to take animal food, if they are not to be overcome and enslaved by others."[88]

To his followers, he recomended:

"Take as much of that (meat) as you can, without fearing criticism. The country has been flooded with dyspeptic Babaji living on vegetables only. That is no sign of Sattva but of deep Tamas—the shadow of death."[89]

---

86. Ibid.,
87. Ibid.,
88. Ibid. p-386.
89. Ibid. p-402.

He himself never observed rules related to eating even as a monk. He was fond of *pan*,(betel) *supari* (betel-nut) tobacco, meat, ice-cream and did not give up all such prohibited food till the end of his life, despite harsh condemnations at the hands of the orthodox hindus. At Madras while countering such orthodox hindus, Vivekananda replied:

"Upon every educated Indian devolves the responsibility of submitting the contents of Dharma to the test. For this reason we must come out of the limited grooves of the past and take a look at the world as it moves onward to progress at the present day. And if we find that there are hide-bound customs which are impeding the growth of our social life or disturbing our philosophical outlook it is time for us to take an advance step by eschewing them."[90]

Once when a representative of the Cow Protection Society sought Vivekanandas support for the cause, the latter refused. When the representative insisted and argued that cow was to be adorned as a mother, Vivekananda retorted, "The cow is indeed our mother otherwise who would have given birth to such a talented son."[91]

In India, people had put up with 'the spiritual authority with a vengeance—one believed in cow only because the word occurred in the Vedas'. People were brain-washed to believe that their forefathers had the wisdom of everything past, present and future. Even modern science could be located in some old Sanskrit verses.[92] Here his ideas are in sharp contrast with that of Swami Dyananda Sarswati who stated in his book 'Satyartha Prakash' that cow was holy and the Vedas were storehouses of all knowledge even modern inventions like steam engines, guns, cannons etc., were shown to have been known to the poets of Vedas.[93] Vivekananda

90. *Reminiscences of Vivekananda-by Eastern & Western Disciples*, Pub-Advaita Ashram, Almora, 1961, Vol-I, p-267.
91. C.W. Vol-VI, 1956, p-450-51.
92. C.W. Vol-II, p-396, 1970.
93. Maharishi Dayananda Sarswati, *Satyartha Prakash* Arya Sahitya Prakashan, p-382.

characterized all those who upheld such views as 'monomaniacs' and advised the people to beware of them. He suggested that the Hindus should not call themselves Hindus as it covers all the inhabitants of India like Mohammedans, Christians, Jains etc, instead, they should call themselves vaidikas, followers of Vedas or the Vedantists, followers of Vedanta.[94]

Despite the ire of the religious reactionaries he boldly expressed his iconoclastic views even in the last days of his life. He desired Hinduism to be dynamic, to discard those religious injunctions which stood for inequalities and unscientific explanation of things. He wanted his countrymen to be rational and to test the religion on the basis of science, and reason and if the former was found in contrast then to give it up. Freedom was his watchword even in the domain of religion.

His assertions that God is not in the temples, man is the creator of God, religion is not in the scriptures, some hindu scriptures are the production of men of low intelligence, cow is not holy, beef-eating is not irreligious, religion should keep off from dictating the life of the individual, were hard to digest by the religious reactionaries. They refused to recognise him as a monk, but monk he was, though iconoclastic.

94. *Lectures from Colombo to Almora*, p-18.

Swami Vivekananda: An Apostle of Harmony

"I Have no word to say against any religion or founder of religion in the world. All religions are sa cred to me."

— **Swami Vivekananda**

Vivekananda rejected rigidity in religions, and opposed orthodoxy, bigotry, sectarianism and fanaticism. He considered them as dangerous diseases, harmful not only for the health of the society and nation but the world at large.

Strongly condemning the above doctrines, he said:

"Sectarianism...and fanaticism had long possessed this beautiful earth. They have filled the earth with violence, drenched it often and often with human blood, destroyed civilization and sent whole nations to despair. Had it not been for these horrible demons, human society would have been far more advanced than it is now."[1]

Characterizing fanaticism as a dangerous concept and its practitioner a lunatic, Vivekananda opined:

"Each religion brings out its own doctrines and insists upon them as being the only true one. And not only does it do that, but it thinks that he who does not believe in them must go to the horrible place. Some will even draw the sword to compel others to believe as they do. This is not through wickedness, but through a particular disease of the human brain called fanaticism... They are quite as irresponsible as other lunatics in the

---

1. C.W. Vol-I, 1947, p-4.

There are fanatics in every society, and women very frequently join in these outcries, because of their impulsive nature. Every fanatic who gets up and denounces something can secure a following. Very easy to break down; a maniac can break anything he likes, but it would be hard for him to build up anything.

Think of the fanatics; they make the longest faces and all their religion is to fight against others in word and act. Think of what they have done in the past, and of what they would do now, if they were given a free hand. They would deluge the whole world in blood tomorrow, if it would give them power.

world. This disease of fanaticism is one of the most dangerous of all diseases. All the wickedness of human nature is roused by it. Anger is stirred up, nerves are strung high, and human beings become like tigers."[2]

A fanatic according to Vivekananda is a maniac who can destroy everything but cannot build anything.

"There are fanatics in every society, and women very frequently join in these outcries, because of their impulsive nature. Every fanatic who gets up and denounces something can secure a following. Very easy to break down; a maniac can break anything he likes, but it would be hard for him to build up anything."[3]

According to him the real motive of fanatics is not religion but to gain power by misusing religion and for it he never hesitates to cause killings.

"Think of the fanatics; they make the longest faces and all their religion is to fight against others in word and act. Think of what they have done in the past, and of what they would do now, if they were given a free hand. They would deluge the whole world in blood tomorrow, if it would give them power."[4]

No civilization can grow unless fanaticism, bloodshed and brutality stop. No civilization can lift up its head until we look charitably upon one another; and the first step towards that much needed charity is to look charitably and kindly upon religious convictions of others...however different our religious ideas and convictions may be."[5]

He stated that it is better to be an atheist than a religious bigot:

"In the matter of religion there were two extremes, the bigot and the atheist. There were some good in the atheists, but the bigot live only for his little self."[6]

2. C.W. Vol-II, 1970, p-377-78.
3. Ibid. p-116.
4. C.W. Vol-IV, 1948, p-9.
5. C.W. Vol-III, 1948, p-188.
6. Marie Louise Burke, *Swami Vivekananda in America—New Discoveries*, Advaita Ashram Calcutta, 1958, p-248.

A religious bigot hates other religions and their believers. He is firm in his convictions and it is impossible to change him. Vivekananda said "I would believe you if you were to say that I could pluck a tooth from the mouth of a crocodile without being bitten, but I cannot believe when you say a bigot can be changed."[7]

Bigotry breeds on ignorance and false belief in the correctness of one's own religion:

"Each religion lays the claim that its particular book is the only authentic word of the God, that all other books are false and are impositions upon poor credulity, and that to follow other religion is to be ignorant and spiritually blind.

Such bigotry is characteristic of the orthodox elements of all sections. For instance, the orthodox followers of the Vedas claim that the Vedas are the only authentic word of the God in the world; that God has spoken to the world only through the Vedas, not only that...But that the world itself exists by virtue of Vedas. Before the world was, the Vedas were there. Everything in the world exists because it is in the Vedas. A cow exists because the name of the cow is mentioned in the Vedas. The language of the Vedas is the original language of the God, all other languages are mere dialects and not of God. Every word and syllable in the Vedas must be pronounced correctly, each sound must be given its true vibration, and every departure from this rigid exactness is a terrible sin and unpardonable."[8]

Strongly condemning bigotry he stated :

"What has bigotry done? It has stalked death in every step, over fertile fields and peaceful homes. It has torn parents from children and children from parents and today its gaunt hand is raised in secret against fellow-citizens and neighbours."[9]

To fanatics, bigots and orthodox, religion is a trade resulting in competition, fighting, selfishness. Thus

7. Ibid., p-651.
8. C.W. Vol-VI, 1956, p-47.
9. Marie Louise Burke, p-256.

forcing them to have a narrow and self-centered outlook, making them distant from spirituality. Whereas a spiritual man's love is all encompassing.[10]

A truly religious person, according to him, does good to others despite his non-belief in God.

"Although a man has not attained a single system of philosophy, although he does not believe in any God and never has believed, although he has not prayed even once in his whole life, if the simple power of good actions has brought him to the state where he is ready to give up his life and all for others, he has arrived at the same point to which the religious man will come through his prayers and the philosopher through his knowledge." [11]

In his views, all those who have actually attained any real religious nature never wrangle over the form in which the different religions are expressed and they don't quarrel with anybody because he does not speak the same tongue.

"Never quarrel about religion. All quarrels and disputations concerning religion simply show that spirituality is not present. Religious quarrels are always over the husks. When purity, when spirituality goes, quarrels begin, and not before."[12]

Explaining the cause of religious struggles, he boldly declared "there runs an economic struggle through every religious struggle. This animal called man has some religious influence but he is guided by economy."[13] No religion preaches hatred, enmity or fights, then who incites the people to do these things? Vivekananda stated in one word 'politics.'[14]

> Never quarrel about religion. All quarrels and disputations concerning religion simply show that spirituality is not present. Religious quarrels are always over the husks. When purity, when spirituality goes, quarrels begin, and not before.

10. Life, Vol-II, p-366.
11. C.W. VI, p-127.
12. Ibid.,
13. C.W. Vol-I, p-454, 1947.
14. C.W. Vol-VI, p-121, 1948.

Abhorring quarrels on the issue of religion, Vivekananda asked his admirers to question those who fight in the name of religion.

"If two men quarrel about religion, just ask them the question: 'Have you seen God? Have you seen these things? One man says that Christ is the only Prophet: well has he seen Christ 'Has your father seen Him? No Sir,....'Then what are you quarrelling for? The fruits have fallen into the ditch, and you are quarrelling over the basket! Sensible men and women should be ashamed to go on quarrelling in that way!"[15]

In answer to a question "why do religious reformers fight with each other?; Vivekananda said "They are like bulls tied to the oil mill 'purposely' blindfolded."[16]

Vivekananda's concept of religion was different. It was not in theory but in practice. To be good and to do good was the gist of his religion.[17] He who only studies books for religion is like the ass who carried a heavy load of sugar on its back, without knowing the sweetness of it. "In my opinion", he said, "books have produced more evil than good. They are accountable for many mischievous doctrines. Creeds all come from books, and books alone are responsible for the prosecution and fanaticism in the world."[18]

"Clinging to books only degenerates the human mind. Was there a more horrible blasphemy than the statement that all the knowledge of God is confined to this or that book? How dare men call infinite, and yet try to compress Him within the covers of a little book! Millions of people have been killed because they did not believe what the books said, because they would not see all the knowledge of God within the covers of a book. Of course this killing and murdering has gone by,

15. C.W. Vol-IV, p-128.
16. *Vivekananda in Indian Newspapers*, p-47.
17. Letters, p-52.
18. C.W. IV, 1948, p-33, 42.

but the world is still tremendously bound up in a belief in books.[19]

Let us give up quarreling over the divergences of doctrines and religions; let us preach the religion of Hope and Cheer. We are all brothers, we have all the same rights. All rivers make their way to the ocean; if as they run downhill, their channels diverge, it is still the same water."[20]

Vivekananda was proud of the fact that numerous sects existed in India. But he was against sectarianism. Speaking before the Indian audience, he said:

"Sects, as a matter of course, must exist here, but what need not exist is sectarian quarrel. Sect must be but sectarianism need not....Our most ancient books have declared: 'That which exists is One; sages call Him by various names. Therefore, if there are these sectarian struggles, if there are these fights among the different sects, if there is jealousy and hatred between the different sects in India, the land where all sects have always been honoured, it is a shame on us who dare to call ourselves the descendants of those fathers."[21]

He knew very well the darker side of the religion. He boldly stated that religions, having tremendous power in them have often done more injury to the world than good, simply on account of their narrowness.[22]

Therefore he advised people to stay away from the organized religions as they are not only narrow but also perpetrators of religious persecutions and brutalities.

"If you want to be religious, enter not the gate of any organized religions. They do a hundred times more evil than good, because they stop the growth of each one's individual development. Study everything, but keep your seat firm. If you take my advice, do not put your neck into the trap. The moment they try to put their

19. C.W. Vol-I, 1947, p-186, 326.
20. Ibid., p-85.
21. C.W. Vol-III, p-372. 1948.
22. C.W. Vol-II, p-68.

noose on you, get your neck out and go somewhere else. As the bee culling honey from many flowers remain free, not bound by any flower, be not bound. Religion is only between you and your God, and no third person must come between you. Think what these organized religions have done! Was Napoleon more terrible than these religious persecutions?..If you and I organize, we begin to hate every person. It is better not to love, if loving only means hating others. That is not love. That is hell! If loving your own people means hating everybody else, it is the quintessence of selfishness and brutality and the effect is that it will make you brutes."[23]

He was the strongest advocate of freedom in every field including religion. He believed that none, even if he be a religious leader, should be allowed to impose his views upon others. A man should think what is good for him.

"Each one thinks his method is best. Very good! But remember it may be good for you. One food, which is very indigestible to one, is very digestible to another.. Because it is good for you, do not jump to the conclusion that your method is everybody's method, that Jack's coat fits John and Mary. All the uneducated, uncultured, unthinking men and women have been put into that sort of Strait Jacket! Think for yourselves. Become atheist! Become materialist! That would be better. Exercise the mind.."[24]

Today laws are being enacted to prevent people from leaving the religion they are born in, and to convert to religion of their choice. Vivekananda was deadly against it. He stated that man should be allowed to choose his own religion.

"One man should not force another to worship what he worships, All attempts to herd together human beings by means of armies, force, or arguments, to drive them pell-mell into the same enclosure and make them

One man should not force another to worship what he worships, All attempts to herd together human beings by means of armies, force, or arguments, to drive them pell-mell into the same enclosure and make them worship the same God have failed and will fail always, because it is constitutionally impossible to do so. Not only so, there is the danger of arresting their growth.

23. Ibid., p-94.
24. Ibid., p-93.

worship the same God have failed and will fail always, because it is constitutionally impossible to do so. Not only so, there is the danger of arresting their growth."[25]

So much so that he did not even approve parents to impose their religion upon their children. He said:

"For instance, when I am a child, my father puts a book into my hand which says God is such and such. What business has he to put that into my mind?[26]

What right has my master or society to put things into my head?...How many beautiful things which would have become wonderful spiritual truths, have been nipped in the bud by this horrible idea of a family religion, a social religion, a national religion, and so forth.[27]

It is good to be born in a church, but it is bad to die there. It is good to be born a child, but bad to remain a child. Churches, ceremonies and symbols are good for children, but when the child is grown he must burst the church or himself. We must not remain children forever. It is like trying to fit one coat to all sizes and growths. I do not deprecate the existence of sects in the world. Wish to God there were twenty million more, for the more there are, the greater the field for selection there will be.[28]

Just as there are certain varieties in human nature, so it is necessary that there should be an equal number of forms in religion; and the more there are, the better for the world. If there are twenty forms of religion in the world, it is very good; if there are four hundred, so much the better—there will be the more to choose from.[29]

Advocating complete freedom in the matter of religion, he declared:

> For instance, when I am a child, my father puts a book into my hand which says God is such and such. What business has he to put that into my mind?

---

25. C.W. Vol-IV, p-55. 1948.
26. Ibid.,
27. Ibid.,
28. Swami Chetnananda ed., *Vedanta: Voice of Freedom* Advaita Ashram, Calcutta, 1991, p-79.
29. C.W. IV, p-37.

"We reject none, neither theist, nor pantheist, monist, polytheist, agonistic, nor atheist, the only thing of being a discipline is modeling a character at once the broadest and the most intense...we leave everybody free to know, select and follow whatever suits and help him."[30]

He said:

"Take up the one which suits you best and preserve in it. This is your Ishta, your special ideal."[31]

Religion must be inclusive and not look down with contempt upon one another. He suggested his followers to encompass a broader spirit towards other religions and their followers.

"We must become many sided, indeed we must become Protean in character, so as not to tolerate, but to do what is more difficult, to sympathise, to enter into other's path, and feel with him in his aspirations and seeking after God."[32]

In the World Parliament of Religions, he presented India as a role model for the entire world. A land of multiple religions, where believers of different religions lived in harmony and which had given shelter to the prosecuted and refugees of all religions and all nations of the earth. He proudly proclaimed in United States:

"Going back to our theories, people in the West came about one hundered years ago to this point, that they must tolerate other religion. But we know that toleration is not sufficient towards other religion, we must accept it. Thus it is not a question of subtraction, it is a question of addition. The truth is the result of all these different sides added together. Each of all these religions represents one side, the fullness being the addition of all these. And so in science, it is addition that is law."[33]

---

30. Bhupendranath Datta, *Swami Vivekananda, Patriot and Prophet*, Navabharat. Press, Calcutta, 1954, p-265.
31. Ibid., p-56.
32. C.W. Vol-VI, 1956, p-138.
33. Marie Louise Burke, p-418-419.

He echoed the same views when he landed at Colombo in January 1897 after his memorable work in the west. Speaking before the hindu community, which had arranged a royal reception for him, he said:

"The great principles underlying all this wonderful, infinite ennobling, expansive view of man and God and the world have been produced in India. In India alone man has not stood up to fight for a little tribal God, saying 'My God is true and yours is not true; let us have a fight over it.' It was only here that such ideas did not occur as fighting for little gods. These great underlying principles, being based upon the eternal nature of man, are as potent today for working for the good of the human race as this earth remains...

And that is exactly what we do in India...It is here in India that Hindus have built and are still building churches for Christians and mosques for the Mohammedan.... we will and must go on building churches for the Christians and mosques for the Mohammedan until we conquer through love, until we have demonstrated to the world that love alone is the fittest thing to survive and not hatred...."[34]

This makes it crystal clear that he had no hatred towards any religion and at the same time did not regard hinduism superior to other religions. His was a way of harmony and not exclusiveness.

At another place he said:

"All religions are so many stages.... they are travelling from truth to truth; they become dangerous only when they become rigid and will not move further—then they cease to grow.[35]

One religion is best adapted to a certain people because of habits of life, association, hereditary habits and climate influences. Another religion is suited to another people for similar reasons...Let the great stream flow on and he is fool who would try to change

All religions are so many stages.... they are travelling from truth to truth; they become dangerous only when they become rigid and will not move further—then they cease to grow.

---

34. *Lectures from Colombo to Almora*, p-13.
35. Marie Louise Burke, p-530.

its course, when nature will work the solution. If there were not different religions, no religion would survive.[36]

Instead of antagonizing, therefore, we must help all such interchange of ideas between different races, by sending teachers to each other, so as to educate humanity in all the various religions of the world; but we must insist as the great Buddhist emperor of India, Ashoka did, in the second century before Christ, not to abuse others, or to try to make a living out of other's faults; but to help, to sympathise, and to enlighten.[37]

For one religion to become the nation's religion would be dangerous and degenerating to man. Following are some of his statements which invariably emphasise variation.

"One religion cannot suit all. Man is the product of two forces, action and reaction which makes him think...and as soon as his thinking power goes, he becomes no better than an animal. Who would like such a man? God forbid that any such state should come upon the people of India. Variety in unity is necessary to keep man as man.[38] We must not seek that all of us should think alike. There would then be no thought to think. We would be all alike, like Egyptian Mummies in a Museum, looking at each other without thought to think.[39]

It is impossible that all difference can cease; it must exist; without variation life must cease. It is this clash, the differentiation of thought that makes for light, for motion, for everything. Differentiation, infinitely contradictory, must remain, but it is not necessary that we should hate each other therefore; it is not necessary therefore that we should fight each other.[40]

...There can never be one religion only, it would be death to all other religions. If everyone thought alike,

One religion cannot suit all. Man is the product of two forces, action and reaction which makes him think...and as soon as his thinking power goes, he becomes no better than an animal. Who would like such a man? God forbid that any such state should come upon the people of India. Variety in unity is necessary to keep man as man.

36. Ibid., p-651.
37. C.W. Vol-IV, 1948, p-376-77.
38. *Lectures from Colombo to Almora*, p-16.
39. C.W. Vol-II, p-363. 1970.
40. C.W. Vol-III, 1948, p-115.

what monotony! Look alike and think alike—what could we do but sit down and die in despair? We cannot live like a row of chipmunks, variation belong to human life.[41]

Variety is the very soul of life. When it dies out entirely, creation will die. When this variation in thought is kept, we must exist; and we need not quarrel because of that variety.[42]

Speaking about himself, Vivekananda stated:

"I do not want to live in a grave like land; I want to be a man in the world of many-variation, the sign of thought. I pray that they (sects) may multiply so that at last there will be many sects as human beliefs— whirlpool and eddies occur only in a rushing living thought. Let each have his individual method of thought in religion."[43]

The idea of universal religion too was dangerous for the mankind:

"If by the idea of the universal religion is meant any one set of doctrines which should be believed in by all mankind, it is impossible; it can never be; any more than there will be a time when all faces will be the same. Again if we accept that there will be one universal mythology, that is also impossible; it cannot be; neither can be there one universal ritual. Such a state can never come into existence; if it ever did, the world would be destroyed because variety is the principal of life. What makes us formed human beings? Differentiation. Perfect balance will be destruction."[44]

He warned his countrymen to stay away from revivalism, as it would harm the unity of the country. He said;

"In the meanwhile, in India there is a tremendous revival of religion. There is a danger ahead as well as glory; for revival sometimes breeds fanaticism,

41. C.W. Vol-IX, p-486.
42. Ibid.,
43. C.W. Vol-II, 1968, p-364.
44. Ibid., p-382.

sometimes goes to the extreme, so that often it is not even in the power of those who start the revival to control it when it has gone beyond a certain length. It is better, therefore, to be forewarned."[45]

"Harmony of religions is the crying need of the day. It is essential to the peace and progress of the world. No civilization can exist or grow without this. All bigotry and intolerance, all narrowness and sectarianism must leave human minds. Instead there should be mutual regard, friendliness and cooperation in all spheres of life. The time has come when religious ideas must broaden."[46]

He disapproved of making a claim of Vedanta's superiority over other religious scriptures. He told a disciple who was impatient with other faiths, "What you mean by Shastras? If you consider the Shastras as the only authority, why not the Bible or the Avesta?" The adamant disciple still argued that others were not as old as the Vedas. Vivekananda replied, "who has given you the right to say that truth exist nowhere else but in Vedas."[47]

His religious ideas were in sharp contrast with Swami Dayananda's views. Dayananda vehemently asserted the superiority of hinduism over all other religions. His call 'back to Vedas' was revivalistic and his attitude towards other religion was venomous. He regarded all religions except hinduism inferior and worthless and insulted their pro-pounders. Sikhism, the religion of sikhs according to Dayananda was without divine light and Guru Nanak was a *dambhi* (Hypocrite) devoid of all scholastic knowledge. He made fun of Guru's opinion about Vedas. Dayananda wrote in his *"Satyartha Prakash"* (Light of Truth) about Guru Nanak's ignorance of Vedas and other scriptures and Sanskrit language. When Dayananda was told about Guru

45. C.W. Vol-III, 1948, p-175.
46. Swami Satprakashnanda, *Swami Vivekananda's Contributions to the Present Age*, Vedanta Society St. Louise, America, 1978 p-146.
47. *Inspired Talks of Vivekananda*, Advaita Ashram, Almora, 1939, p-32.

Nanak's verses in which the latter had mentioned Vedas, Dayananda pointed out:

"However, he (Guru Nanak) might have passed as Sanskrit scholar by making those Sanskrit verses among the villagers who had never heard a word of Sanskrit before. He would have never done it but for his desire for popularity, honor and fame. It is on this account that the calumniation and praise of Vedas are found here and there in his book; for had he not done so, some one would ask the meaning of Vedas, and had he not been able to tell it, he would have lost his respect."[48]

Swami Dayanand asked the Sikhs to give up Sikhism. He stated that if the Sikhs give up sensuousness and wicked pride and promote the Vedic religion, they would do a world of good.[49]

Arya Samachar, published from Lahore lampooned Sikhism as:

> *Nanak Shah fakeer ne naya chalaya panth,*
> *Idhar udhar se jod kar likh mara ik Granth*
> *Pehlay chely kar liye, peechey badla bhes*
> *Sar pe safa bandh kar, rakh leeny sab kes.*

(Nanak launched a new faith and wrote a scripture by joining fragments of different religions. First he made his disciples and later changed his guise, wound a turban and sported a beared.)

Dayananda was highly critical of Kabir Panth calling it 'a child's play' and its followers as 'ignorant fellows fell into the snare.' Dadu, founder of Dadu Panth, according to Dayananda was 'ignorant', Ram Charan, founder of Ram Sanehi Faith an 'artless clown' and his faith as 'nonsense'. He did not spare any religion. Strongly

48. Dayananda Sarswati, *Satyartha Prakasha* English translation by Durga Prasad, Jan Gyan Prakashan N.D. 1970, p-356.
49. Ibid.,

condemning *Narayanism* and *Gosainism*, Swami Dayananda, called their founders 'fraud' and 'cheat.'[50]

Calling Prophet Mohammed 'a voluptuous' and not learned, Dayananda stated that Koran lacked divine light. 'It cannot be made by God; it appears to have been written by bewildered mind' and is 'not a book of wisdom'.He charged Islam with violence, slaughter and love of loot.

The acrimonious tone and manner adopted by Swami Dayananda in the criticism of other creeds was resented not only by the believers of those religions but also by a large section of hindus who were unorthodox and believed in synthesis. Besides, it led to communal divide and communal violence. In Amritsar when Dayananda glorified hinduism and belittled Sikhism, Sikhs responded by threatening to assassinate him.[51] Vivekananda too was critical of Swami Dayananda's glorification of ancient India and assertion of superiority of hinduism over all other religions.

"There were many good things in ancient times, but there were bad things too. The good things are to be retained but the India that is to be, the future India, must be greater than the ancient India."[52]

Hate only degenerates and take down the man as well as the nation downwards.

Whatever cloak ancient or modern sophistry may try to overthrow it, the inevitable result—the vindication of the moral law, that none can hate others without degenerating himself—is that the race that was foremost amongst the ancient races is now a bye-word, and a scorn among nations.[53]

"...If anybody dreams of the exclusive survival of his own religion and the destruction of others, I pity on him from the bottom of my heart, and point out to him that upon the banner of every religion will soon be

50. Ibid., p-358, 359.
51. Kenneth W. Jones, *Arya Dharma*, Manohar, N.D. 1976, p-40.
52. *Letters of Swami Vivekananda*, Advaita Ashram, 1946, p-252.
53. C.W. Vol-IV, 1948, p-310.

written, in spite of his resistance, 'Help and Not Fight', 'Assimilation and Not Destruction', 'Harmony and Peace and Not Dissension.[54]

Why take a single instrument from the great religious orchestra of the earth? Let the great symphony go on. Be pure... give up superstition and see the wonderful harmony of nature...All the religions are good since the essentials are the same. Each individual should have the perfect exercise of his individuality, but these individualities form a perfect whole...Each creed has something to add to the wonderful structure.[55]

Explaining his attitude towards all the religions, he said:

"my attitude towards all of them is one of extreme sympathy, my teaching is antagonistic to none.[56]

"I accept all religions...I shall go to the mosque of Mohammedan, I shall enter the Christian church and kneel before the Crucifix, I shall enter the Buddhist temple...I shall go into the forest and sit down in meditation with the Hindus.

Acceptance—not even toleration which is an insult and a blasphemy.[57]

"We have to learn that all religions, under whatever name, they may be called, either Hindu, Buddhist, Mohammedans or Christian, have the same God, and he who derides any one of these derides his own God."[58]

He never asked people to give up their respective faiths, but on the contrary he advised them to act sincerely in their own beliefs. All the religions of the earth, he thought, were so many different ways to reach the same destination.

> I accept all religions...I shall go to the Mosque of Mohammedan, I shall enter the Christian church and kneel before the Crucifix, I shall enter the Buddhist temple...I shall go into the forest and sit down in meditation with the Hindus.

54. *The Life of Swami Vivekananda*, by Eastern & Western Disciples, Pub-Advaita Ashram, Almora, Vol-I, p-303. Also see. C.W. Vol-I, p-24.
55. *Vivekananda in Indian Newspapers*, ed. by Sankri Prasad Basu & Sunil Bihari Ghose, Pub-Bookland, Calcutta 1969, p-23.
56. Ibid., p-82.
57. C.W. Vol-II, p-374, 1968.
58. *A Book of India*, ed. by B.N. Pandey, Pub-Collins, London 1965, p-296.

He revered all the sufi and bhakti saints like Guru Nanak, Dadu, Kabir as they preached the real religion , religion based on equality and love for mankind. Speaking about these saints, Vivekananda remarked:

"...These Messengers must have come from God, else how could they have been so great? You look at every defect. Each one of us has his defects. The wickeds are always looking for defects...Flies come and seek for the ulcer and the bees come only for the honey in the flower. Do not follow the ways of the flies but that of the bees."[59]

Unlike Swami Dayananda, Vivekananda had high opinion of Islam.

"My experience is that if ever any religion approached to equality in an appreciable manner it is Islam and Islam alone.[60]

He had studied Koran and openly declared, "There is one thing very remarkable about Koran. Even to this day, it exists as it was found eleven hundred years ago. It retains its pristine purity and is free from interpolations." [61]

> There is one thing very remarkable about Koran. Even to this day, it exists as it was found eleven hundred years ago. It retains its pristine purity and is free from interpolations.

In an answer to a question, "what was good in Islam? Vivekananda replied:

"If there was no good, how could it live? The good alone lives. Mohammed was the Prophet of equality, of brotherhood of man, the brotherhood of Mussalmans...Mohammed by his life showed that amongst Mohammedan there should be perfect equality and brotherhood. There was no question of race, caste or creed, colour or sex. The Sultan of Turkey may buy a Negro from the mart of Africa and bring him in chains to Turkey; but should he become a Mohammedan and have a sufficient merit and abilities, he might even marry the daughter of the sultan."[62] He also praised Islam because unlike Hinduism the priest

59. C.W. Vol-I, p-482.

60. *Life*, Vol-I, p-265. 1979.

61. Ibid.,

62. C.W. Vol-IV, 1948, p-129-30.

It is the only religion that has completely broken down the idea of priest. The leader of the prayers stand with the back to the people, and only the reading of the Koran may take place from the pulpit.

What Mohammed did was to limit a man to four wives; polygamy in a far worse form was already practised in Arabia.

has no role to play as mediator between the individual and God.

"It is the only religion that has completely broken down the idea of priest. The leader of the prayers stand with the back to the people, and only the reading of the Koran may take place from the pulpit."[63]

In *Satyarth Prakasha*, Swami Dayananda minced no words in maligning the Prophet on the issue of Polygamy but Vivekananda admired the Prophet and explained the reason for such advocacy by saying that before Islam polygamy in worse form existed in Arabia.

"What Mohammed did was to limit a man to four wives; polygamy in a far worse form was already practised in Arabia."[64]

In America, he rebuked a person who criticized Islam on the ground that women had not been given any rights. Vivekananda pointed out sharply that muslim women had certain rights not even enjoyed by the so-called free American women.[65]

Vivekananda found Islam more liberal than all other religions including Hinduism and Christianity. Speaking before a congregation in America, he pointed out the strong points of Islam as:

"Compare this with the way in which the Negroes and the American Indians are treated in this country! And what do Hindus do? If one of your missionaries chance to touch the food of an orthodox person, he would throw it away. Notwithstanding our grand philosophy, you note our weakness in practice; but there you see the greatness of the Mohammedan beyond other races showing itself in equality, perfect equality regardless of race or colour."[66]

The Swami wanted the Islamic democratic and aggressive spirit to be instilled into metaphysical

63. *Notes of Some wandering with Swami Vivekananda*, Sister Nivedita, p-121.
64. *Reminiscences of Vivekananda*, Advaita Ashram Calcutta, 1961, p-193.
65. Ibid.,
66. C.W. Vol-IV, 1948, p-130.

concepts of hinduism. " There I am firmly persuaded that without the help of practical Islam, theories of Vedantism, however fine and wonderful they may be, are entirely valueless to the vast mass of mankind. We want to lead mankind to the place where there is neither the Vedas, nor the Bible, nor the Koran; yet this has to be done by harmonising the Vedas, the Bible and the Koran."[67]

A lay disciple said to swami: "It is too difficult a task to establish harmony and cooperation among all the varying religious sects and creeds that are current in the country and make them act in unison for a common purpose" swami cried out in excited voice, "Don't come here any more if you think any task too difficult."[68]

He emphasized:

"For our own motherland a junction of the two great systems, Hinduism and Islam—Vedanta brain and Islam body is the only hope.[69]

The hindu can worship any sage and any saint from any country whatsoever, and as a fact we know that we go and worship many times in the churches of the Christians, and many, a many times in the Mohammedan mosques, and that is good. Why not? Ours...is the universal religion. It is inclusive enough, it is broad enough to include all the ideals."[70]

On one occasion, he said:

"That will be the greatest period of the Indian history when on the steps of a temple an atheist will preach against temple worship and no body will harm him. That is my conviction. I go to a temple that is my conviction. If he criticizes it that is his conviction."[71]

That will be the greatest period of the Indian history when on the steps of a temple an atheist will preach against temple worship and no body will harm him. That is my conviction. I go to a temple that is my conviction. If he criticizes it that is his conviction.

67. C.W. Vol-VI, 1956, p-415.
68. *Last Days of Vivekananda*- Eastern & Western Disciples, Advaita Ashram Calcutta, 1927, p-59
69. C.W. Vol-VI, 1956, p-416.
70. C.W. Vol-III 1948, p-253.
71. *Centenary of Vivekananda's Participation of the Chicago Parliament of Religions*, Pub- R.K. Mission, N.D. 1993, p-15.

With in one's own
family there could
be members of
various faiths. A
Muslim father could
have a Christian
wife and a
Buddhist son if
each one so
desired. As in all
other spheres of
life there could be
unity in diversity in
religious beliefs
within the same
family.

Diversity in religions and the harmonious co-existence of the followers of different faiths according to Vivekananda was the strongest strength of India.

"Within one's own family there could be members of various faiths. A muslim father could have a christian wife and a buddhist son if each one so desired. As in all other spheres of life there could be unity in diversity in religious beliefs within the same family."[72]

He presented a vision of a true universal religion, which would be the mixture of all the religions to raise humanity to its rightful place:

" ...It will not be Brahminic or Buddhistic, or Christian or Mohammedan, but the sum total of these, and still have infinite space for development, which in its catholicity will embrace in its infinite arms, and find a place for every human being, from the lowest grovelling savage not far removed from the brute, to the highest man towering by the virtues of his head and heart almost above humanity, making society stand in awe of him and doubt his human nature. It will be a religion which will have no place for persecution or intolerance in its polity, which will recognise divinity in every man and woman and whose whole scope, whose whole force, will be centered in aiding humanity to realise its own true divine nature."[73]

Vivekananda had a plan to bring Hindus, Muslims, Sikhs and Christians together under one religious banner. K. Sundrarama who met the Swami at Madras reminisces the lecture of Vivekananda in which the latter explained his plan for the vast religious reformation in India which would serve to bring Hindus, Christians, Mohammedans, Buddhists and all other under a common flag of brotherly union and serve as a star of hope and harmony and a ceaseless incentive to the striving by men of all creeds and colours after a common goal of national aspiration. He wanted a new sort and style of temple with a hall in the

72. C.W. Vol-VIII, 1959, p-254.
73. C.W. Vol-VII, p-19.

front containing statues of the sages and prophets of all great religions and behind it an inner precinct containing a pillar with the letter *om* inscribed on it underneath the open sky.[74]

One can find in the architecture of Ramakrishna Temple at Belur Math, contemplated by Vivekananda, a blending of Hindu temple, Muslim mosque and Christian church.

Thus spirituality advocated by Vivekananda was not related with hinduism only, it was the sum total of spiritual values contained in all the Indian religions and sects.

He was an apostle of Hindu-Muslim brotherhood and regarded the two as the sons of Mother India. According to Vivekananda's disciples, Vivekanand's views regarding hindu-muslim unity underwent change during his travels. About distinction between the two he, "as a young man thought to be insuperable barriers to a unified Indian consciousness, were entirely modified and in many sense obliterated."[75]

But the study of his pre-monk life reveals that the secular values were ingrained in him since his childhood. His upbringing in the secular atmosphere at home, his scientific education, his regard and admiration for Kesab Chandra Sen and his Brahmo Samaj training and the lack of communal animosities in the bengali common people and later, the teachings of his Master Swami Ramakrishana made him secular to the core. During his travels, he observed that there was unity in diversity and the alleged difference between hindus and muslims were merely apparent. "For his own personal experience he had seen that the Mohammedan as a race were as generous and as human and as Indian at heart as the Hindu...."[76]

According to Sister Nivedita who observed him closely, the Swami was proud of India's oneness and the

74. *Reminiscences of Vivekananda*, p-97.

75. *Life*, Vol-I, 1979, p-226, 27.

76. Ibid., p-357.

asiatic civilization that "many times on meeting a Mohammedan, he would salute him with the greatest respect, for he would see in him the representative of Asiatic civilization."[77] He could comprehend and defend the grandeur of Chengiz Khan and his dream of Asiatic unity. It was unjust and incorrect to portray Chengiz as 'vulgar aggressor' he was a great soul.[78]

Unlike those who today regard him as their mentor, he had no hatred for mohammedan rule. Infact, he did not consider the muslim conquest as a foreign conquest, for the muslims had become Indians and under them a synthesis of Indian culture had been brought out. He eulogized the liberal spirit of the muslim rulers. "Even to the Mohammedan Rule we owe that great blessing, the destruction of exclusive privilege….The Moham-medan conquest of India came as a salvation to the downtrodden, to the poor. That is why one-fifth of our people have become Mohammedan. It was not the sword that did it all. It would be the height of madness to think it was all the work of sword and fire."[79]

According to him conversion of Hindus to Islam took place to escape from exploitation and injustices. He asked the hindus to ponder over:

> "Why amongst the poor of India are so many Mohammedans. It is nonsense to say they are converted by the sword. It was to gain their liberty from zamindars and from the priests. And as a consequence you find in Bengal there are more Mohammedans than Hindus amongst the cultivators, because there were so many zamindars there."[80]

He also belied the arguments that in the middle ages the hindu women were kept indoors, deprived of education because of the fear of the muslims. He referred Sir William Hunter 'History of the English People' wherein he wrote that hindu women were given

[Sidebar text:]

Even to the Mohammedan Rule we owe that great blessing, the destruction of exclusive privilege….The Mohammedan conquest of India came as a salvation to the downtrodden, to the poor. That is why one-fifth of our people have become Mohammedan. It was not the sword that did it all. It would be the height of madness to think it was all the work of sword and fire.

---

77. Ibid.,
78. Sister Nivedita-*Notes of Some wandering*, p-74.
79. C.W. Vol-III, 1948, p-294.
80. C.W. Vol-VIII, 1959, p-330.

education and some of them could even calculate a solar eclipse.[81]

The Mughal Empire fired and fascinated him. In the words of Sister Christine, 'The Mughals seemed to have cast a spell over the Swami. He depicted this period of Indian history with such dramatic intensity, that the idea often came to us that he was perhaps telling the story of his own past."[82]

He admired Babur, the emperor of India, who although an alien and invader, identified himself with the country and began at once to make roads, plant trees, dig wells and build cities.[83] He placed Akbar in the category of Ramachandra and whenever he spoke of Akbar, who acording to Vivekananda possessed God like qualities, tears came into his eyes.[84] He used to sing before his European disciples the song of Tansen, the poet laureate of the emperor:

Seated on the throne, a God amongst men
Though, the emperor of Delhi.
Blessed was the hour, the minute, the second,
When thou ascended the throne,
O God amongst men,
Thou the Lord of Delhi.
Long live thy crown, thy sceptre, thy throne,
O God amongst men,
Thou Emperor of Delhi.
Live long and remain awakened always,
O son of Humanyoon,
Joy of the sun, God amongst men,
Thou the Emperor of Delhi![85]

His disciples saw him speaking with a burst of enthusiasm on Mughal Emperor Shah Jahan:

---

81. Marie Louise Burke, p-416.
82. *Reminiscences of Vivekananda*, p-188.
83. Sister Nivedita, *The Master As I Saw Him*, p-13.
84. C.W. Vol-IV, 1948, p-374.
85. C.W. Vol-IV, p-394.

"Ah! He was the glory of his line! A feeling for and discrimination of beauty are unparalleled in history. And an artist himself! I have seen a manuscript illuminated by him, which is one of the art treasures of India. What a genius!"[86]

Sister Nivedita writes:

"In these talks of his, the heroism of the Rajput, the faith of the Sikhs, the courage of the Marrattas, the devotion of the saints and the purity of and steadfastness of the noble women, all lived again. Nor would he permit that the Mohammedan should be passed over. Humanyoon, Sher Shah, Akbar, Shah Jahan, each of these, and a hundred more, found a day and a place in his beadroll of glistening names. Now it was that coronation song of Akbar, which is still sung in the streets of Delhi, that he would give us, in every tone and rhythm of Tansena. Again he would explain how the widows of the Mughal house never remarried, but lived like hindu women, absorbed in the worship or in study, through the lonely years. At another place, he would talk of the great national genius that decreed the birth of Indian sovereigns to be of a muslim father and a hindu mother. And yet he would hold us breathless, as we lived through with him the bright, but ill-starred reign of Siraj-ud-daulah, as we heard the exclamation at Plassy of the Hindu General. Listening to an order sent in treachery, 'This is the day lost!' and saw him plunge, with his horse, into the Ganges."[87]

He appreciated the Mughal rulers for the service they had done, not only in exalting the social rights of the lowly-born but also in conserving and developing, in too gentle a race, the ideals of organised struggle and resistance.[88]

He was secular to the core and unbiased in the interpretation of the Indian history unlike the present day reactionaries who are not prepared to accept any

86. Ibid., p-344.
87. Sister Nivedita, *The Master As I Saw Him*, p-52.
88. Ibid. p-246.

criticism of the rulers of their respective communities. In his lecture on Historical Evolution of India, he boldly stated that the rule of Marattas was reactionary and represented fanaticism.

"But the spiritual aspiration that preceeded the rise of the Marattas or Sikh empires was entirely reactionary. We seek in vain to find in the court of Poona or Lahore even a ray of reflection of that intellectual glory which surrounded the courts of the Mughals...It was intellectually the darkest period of the history and both these empires, representing the upheaval of mass fanaticism and hating culture with all their hearts, lost all their motive power as soon as they had succeeded in destroying the rule of the hated Mohammedans."[89]

Sister Christine writes in her reminiscences:

"To him India was not the land of Hindus only, it included all. 'My brother the Mohammedan' was a phrase he often used. For the culture, religious devotion, and virility of these Mohammedan brothers, he had an understanding, an admiration, a feeling of oneness which few Muslims could excel."[90]

Today, the communalists call the muslims the foreigners, the Swami had different views in this regard. In the words of sister Nivedita:

"He constantly pointed out that Mohammadanism had its four fold 'castes—Syyed, Pathan, Moghal and Sheikh—and that of these Sheikhs had an inherited right to the Indian soil and the Indian memory, as ancient and as indisputable as those of any hindu. He told a disciple, a propos of an indiscreetly-written word that Shah Jahan would have turned in his grave to hear himself called a 'foreigner."[91]

She narrates how when she and other disciples of the swami were visiting the Amarnath cave, many muslim pilgrims accompanied him. They along with the Swami

89. See for detail his lectures on Historical Evolution of India, in Vol-VI
90. *Reminiscences* of Swami Vivekananda p-192.
91. Sister Nivedita, The Master. As I Saw Him... p-246.

and other hindu worshippers entered the shrine for pilgrimage. The Tehsildar of that place, who was a muslim and had worshipped in the shrine, afterwards with a group of friends, became the swami's disciple.[92]

He admired the Indian heritage and highly appreciated the magnificent buildings made by the Mughal emperors. During his travels, he also visited Agra. The beauty of Taj Mahal overpowered him. He visited it many times, seeing it from different angles; in every light and remarked: "Every square inch of this wondrous edifice is worth a whole day's patient observation, and it requires at least six months to make a real study of it."[93]

In Lucknow, he was fascinated by the splendour bequeathed by the Nawabs of Oudh, by the city gardens and mosques. In Ajmer, he went to see the palace of Akbar and the Dargah of renowned sufi-saint, Moin-ud-din Chisti. At Hyderabad, he visited Mecca Masjid and the tomb of a famous saint Baba Sarauddin.[94]

He regarded both the Aryans as well as the Mongolians as his ancestors. He proclaimed:

"If I am grateful to my white-skinned Aryan ancestor, I am far more so to my yellow-skinned Mongolian ancestor, and most of all to the black-skinned Negritoid!"[95]

"The Swami" in the words of Sister Nivedita "was immensely proud of his physiognomy of what he called his" Mongolian Jaw, 'regarding it as a sign of bull-dog tenacity of purpose.' One day, he exclaimed, 'Don't you see? The Tartar is the wine of the race! He gives energy and power to every blood!"[96] His liberal religious ideas and secular approach attracted unorthodox elements from every religion including the muslims. They were seen in his congregation and some became his disciples

> If I am grateful to my white-skinned Aryan ancestor, I am far more so to my yellow-skinned Mongolian ancestor, and most of all to the black-skinned Negritoid

---

92. Ibid., p-122.
93. *Life*, Vol-I, 1979, p-217.
94. Ibid., p-279, 375.
95. Sister Nivedita, The Master—As I Saw Him, p-225.
96. Ibid.,

too. One of his greatest admirers at Alwar was a Maulvi Saheb, a teacher of Urdu and Persian. The Maulvi was so impressed by Swami's knowledge and respect for Koran that he informed all his friends who also attended his lectures and became Swami's admirers. The Swami visited the Maulvis' house and dined there.[97]

At Mt. Abu, he stayed in a bungalow of a muslim *vakil* of the state. When asked by a hindu 'How is it, swamiji, that you, a Hindu sanyasi, are living with a Mohammedan?' The swami flared up, 'Sir what do you mean? I am a Sanyasi. I am above social conventions. I can dine even with a Bhangi. Your people and your society may not like but God sanctions it and the scriptures approve it. I see Brahmin everywhere—for me there is nothing high or low, no caste no rank."[98] A muslim gentleman was so influenced by the Swami that he named himself Mohammedananda.[99]

He often narrated an incident when his life was saved by a muslim cemetery keeper—He was in Almora and had fainted because of hunger. He was lying opposite the cemetery for many hours when the keeper found him and gave him cucumbers to eat.[100]

At Hyderabad, a hearty welcome was accorded to him by the state dignatries. Five hundered people including Shams-ul-Ulema Syed Ali Bilgrami, Nawab Imam Jung Bahadur, Nawab Dula Khan Bahadur, Nawab Imdad Nawaz, Nawab Secunder Nawaz received him at the station. During his stay in the city, he was the guest of the Nizam of Hyderabad who was well known for catholicity of his views and had visited all the places of Hindu pilgrimage from the Himalayas to Cape-Comorin... When the Swami told the Nawab about his intention to visit America, the latter immediately promised to pay Rs.1,000 towards his expense.[101]

97. *Life*, Vol-I, p-267.
98. Ibid.,
99. V.K. Rao, *Swami Vivekananda*, Publication Division, N.D. 1979 p-240.
100. *Life*, Vol-I, p-250.
101. Ibid., p-375.

He saw his God or Goddess in every being. He worshipped the little daughter of his muslim boatman in Kashmir as the symbol of the divine mother. [102]

During his visit to Punjab after his return from west, a large number of people gathered to welcome him and attended the congregations. At Lahore, Rawalpindi, Sialkot Sanatanna Dharma Sabha and Arya Samaj arranged grand receptions in honour of the Swami and the latter in every such meeting asked the hindus and the muslims to unite. Particularly he asked the *Arya* Samajist to root out the antagonism between the two communities. At Ambala, he made it a point to visit the Hindu-Muslim School because to him it was a symbol of the spirit of unity between the two communities.[103] Seeing his popularity, the Arya Samajist tried to have him in their fold but the he declined on the ground of orthodoxy of the Samajists.[104]

Though like the Arya Samajists, Vivekananda too regarded religion as the backbone of the national life yet his religion was not sectarian and the Ramakrishna Mission did not practise conversion.

The Christian is not to become a Hindu or a Buddhist, nor a Hindu or Buddhist to become a Christian. But each must assimilate the spirit of others and yet preserve its individuality and grow according to its own law of growth.

"The Christian is not to become a Hindu or a Buddhist, nor a Hindu or Buddhist to become a Christian. But each must assimilate the spirit of others and yet preserve its individuality and grow according to its own law of growth."[105]

In India and abroad, wherever he spoke his ideas cast a hypnotic spell over the liberal minded believers and non-believers. Helen Huttington wrote from Brooklyn to the editor of *Brahmavadin* on 2nd March 1896:

"The swami has preached to us a religion that knows no bounds of creeds or dogmas, is uplifting, purifying, infinitely comforting, and altogether without blemish;

102. Sister Nivedita, *Notes of Some Wandering....* p-1280.
103. *Swami Vivekananda and the Modernization of Hinduism* ed. by William Radice, Oxford University press N.D. 1998, p-290.
104. Dhar, p-1018.
105. Marie Louise Burke, p-91. C.W. Vol-I, p-24.

based on the love of the God and man on absolute chastity. By accepting his teachings we do not refute the Christian religion. We only break through the barriers of creeds and old superstitions that ignorant men have raised to shut us off from the God's ineffable presence."[106]

In England, Vivekananda's catholic religious philosophy won admiration, a warm farewell reception was given to the Swami at the time of his departure. It was reported in the Indian Mirror on January 7, 1897:

"If Swami Vivekananda's work here may be called a missionary effort, it may be contrasted with most of the other missionary efforts of the day by its not having produced any bitterness, by its not having given rise to a single instance of ill-feeling or sectarianism. The reason of this is simple, and great is its strength. The swami is not a sectarian; he is the promoter of religion, not of one religion only. The exponents of single points in the vast field of religion can find nothing in him to fight."[107]

Religious labels were to him the handmaidens of narrowness and narrowness the cause of dissension. He told his disciples, "these names Hindu, Christian etc., stand as great bars to all brotherly feelings between man and man."[108]

The true message of religion according to Vivekananda is the idea of unity.

"It is the eternal ground idea of the Spiritual oneness of the whole universe...the only infinite reality, that exist in you and me and in all, in the self, in the soul. The infinite oneness of the soul is the eternal sanction of all morality, that you and I are not only brothers...but that you and I am really one."[109]

Thus Vivekananda was liberal and progressive in his outlook and philosophy, his approach to socio-religious issues was secular. He was bold and never hesitated to

---

106. *Vivekananda in Indian Newspapers*, p-93.
107. Ibid., p-121.
108. Ibid., p-652.
109. Ibid.,

voice his opposition against orthodoxy and hypocrisy of various religions particularly of hinduism. For this he faced fierce criticism and confrontation from the hindu orthodox camp. Paper *Bangabasi* and *Dharamprachark* (newspapers), the organ of the Bharatvarshiya Arya Dharma Pracharak Sabha launched a campaign against the Swami. They attacked his sainthood on the ground of his birth, views and deeds. According to them Vivekananda was not a brahmin and beside, did not act according to the rules, prescribed for the monk by the Sashtras. They argued that for a hindu, conformity to Smriti (rites) was of utmost importance. In other words the Swami was not a hindu, as he did not observe the smriti. So much so that it was difficult to get a distinguished man to preside at a meeting in the Town Hall in Calcutta on September 5, 1894 for the purpose of thanking him for his services to hinduism in America. One of the gentlemen, who was approached for the purpose, a judge of the High Court who was a brahmin, declined saying, "The name of Vivekananda was not given to him by a guru. Moreover according to shastras, a Shudra has no right to be initiated as a monk."[110] The meeting, ultimately was presided over by Raja Peary Mohan Mukherji, a Brahmin, though he agreed to address the meeting he referred to Swamiji as 'Brother Vivekananda.'[111]

Besides, they never hesitated to humiliate him in the presence of his desciples. In April 1897, Raja Ajit Singh of Khetri, a disciple of Vivekananda visited Bengal. The Swami took the Raja to the temples of *Kali* and *Radhakanta* at Dakshineswar. The Raja was welcomed and presented with an auspicious coconut and sacred thread but Swamiji was driven out of the temple. Trilokyanath Biswas, the then keeper of the Dakshineswar temple, did not receive the guests in person and later wrote to the editor of a bengali

110. Ibid., p-50.
111. Ibid.,

newspaper (an English translation of the letter appeared in the Indian Mirror of 4th April 1897) that he did not want to keep any contact with a person who had crossed the ocean and yet called himself a Hindu. He had also ordered a purification puja for the Goddess defiled by the visit of such a person.[112]

The swami was not allowed to celebrate Ramakrishna's birthday festival at Rasmani garden, the proprietors of the garden questioned his religiosity.

The orthodox also objected over Vivekananda's close association with his European disciples. The Swami's foreign disciples were called 'maleccha party'. Vivekananda resented this orthodoxy and the resultant opposition. He vent out his anger over such suffocating religiosity in a letter: "In India the moment I landed they made me shave my head and wear Kaupina with the result that I got diabetes."[113]

> In India the moment I landed they made me shave my head and wear Kaupina with the result that I got diabetes.

However, practical compulsion led him to relent. In those days Belur *Math* was being constructed and in order to save it from the wrath of the orthodox in form of social boycott, Vivekananda decided to follow the traditional norms. Durga puja was celebrated (1901) with true *tantric* rites with sumptuous feeding of local brahmins and the symbolic reconsecration of visitors was organized. The meals for the foreign disciples could be served only at a secluded spot. Mrs. Ole Bull's name, initially proposed for the Executive Committee of the Belur *Math* by Vivekananda himself, had to be dropped. Later the orthodoxy relented and finally accepted that the monks were truly hindu sanyasis.[114]

However, he instructed his followers " to become broad, to go out, to amalgamate, to universalize ..."[115] He revealed to them that the *Math* that was being built would be a centre of liberal ideas. It would harmonize

112. Ibid., p-191.
113. Letters, p-432.
114. Amiya Sen, *History of Ramakrishna Mission*, p-328.
115. C.W. Vol-III 1948, p-271.

The *Math* that was being built would be a centre of liberal ideas. It would harmonize all creeds and all standpoints and "the blazing light of universal harmony that will emanate from here will flood the whole universe."

all creeds and all standpoints and "the blazing light of universal harmony that will emanate from here will flood the whole universe."[116]

He appealed to all his countrymen and the world community at large, irrespective of race, religion, region, caste or creed to launch a struggle to set up a new system based on moral values i.e., on true spiritualism devoid of religious intolerance, persecutions, sectarianism, fanaticism and bigotry and to hand down to future generations an ideal world based on the harmony of religions and nations.

116. C.W. Vol-VII, 1947, p-160.

A Passionate Patriot

*"For the next fifty years this alone be our key–note—this our great
Mother India, let all other vain gods disappear for that time from our minds."*

— Swami Vivekananda

Vivekananda was a patriot-prophet. He was proud to be an Indian and deeply loved his motherland. He regarded its air and dust holy and its land as the place of pilgrimage.

Sister Nivedita, who had observed him closely during the years 1898 to 1902, writes, "Vivekananda was the greatest of nationalists. 'India was Swamiji's greatest passion. India throbbed in his breast, India beats in his pulses, India was his day dream. India was his nightmare. Not only that he himself became India. He was the embodiment of India in flesh and blood".[1] According to Reeves Calkins, "Vivekananda was a patriot much more than a philosopher. I think his passion for the Vedantic propaganda was because this seemed to him the surest way of fostering Indian nationhood."[2] Florence Mishun writing for the Encyclopaedia of the Social Sciences fully endorses the above view when she says: "Vivekananda was in a sense the unconscious Prophet of the new Indian nationalism, whose ideology shows the impress of his doctrine."[3]

Tilak, the leader of India's militant nationalist movement and the one who knew Vivekananda closely

1. C.W. Vol-III, 1948, p-309.
2. *Reminiscences of Vivekananda*, Eastern & Western Disciples Advaita Ashram, Calcutta, 1961, p-388.
3. Santi L. Mukherjee, *The Philosophy of Man-Making*, New Oriental Book Agency, Calcutta, 1971, p-197.

described him as "the real father of Indian nationalism." He was characterized as "Dynamite" by Aurobindo Ghose, and "Prophet of Nationalism" by Bipin Chandra Pal, the two well-known revolutionaries of Bengal.[4] In the words of Netaji Subhash Chandra Bose, "Though the swami never gave any political message, everyone who came into contact with him or his writings developed a spirit of patriotism and political mentality."[5]

Though he did not directly launch or led any political movement, yet his writings and lectures given on religion, inculcated patriotic feelings which in turn gave rise to a revolutionary nationalist movement in India. He chose this way deliberately as he himself pointed out, "If you want to speak of politics in India, you must speak through the language of religion. Unless you put that way they will not listen to you."[6] Later Gandhiji followed the same route to reach the masses.

Vivekananda was born six years after the failure of the revolt of 1857. East India Company's rule had been replaced by the British Queen but as far as the exploitation, oppression and repression of the people and the country was concerned, it had increased many-fold. Indians were considered inferior and the new rulers were bent upon ruling India with an iron hand. In 1876, the age for Indian students appearing for the ICS examination was lowered, besides the Indians were deprived of keeping arms even for their self-defence under the Arms Act of 1878. In the same year, the Vernacular Press Act snatched whatever little freedom the Indian Press had. Entire Bengal, especially Calcutta, which was also the seat of the Government, burnt with indignation. Educated Bengali youth raised a storm of opposition against all these Acts and its maker, Lord Lytton, the then Viceroy of India. Calcutta student community became a honeycomb of secret organisations.

---

4. *The Indian Awakening and Bengal* p-167.
5. S.C. Bose, *Indian Struggle* p-35.
6. C.W. Vol-VIII, p-77.

Surenderanath Banerji[7], a popular professor and the idol of the students was the president of these groups. He raised "the storm in the College Square with his oration on Mazzini, the New Italy Movement and the American War of Independence."[8] Vivekananda, then a school lad, was swayed by the patriotic zeal of Surenderanath Banerji and regularly attended the meetings, listening to the leader with rapt attention.[9]

To contribute to the national cause, Vivekananda joined the Brahmo Samaj, a patriotic organization, but its slow pace could not retain him in its fold for long. His restless nature drove him further on. In 1882, he read Bankim Chandra's novel, *Anand Math*. *Anand Math* depicts hindu sanyasins going out on the pretext of pilgrimage, which gave them protection; and when they had gathered a large number of followers and also enough weaponry, they throw off the pilgrim mask and engage openly in fight. Young Vivekananda was fascinated with sanyasins fighting a revolutionary battle against the oppressors. This seems to have left a lasting impression on his mind. The *Bande Matram* Song, i.e., worship of motherland shook the very core of his being. In future, he enacted the same novel in real life, he became a monk, wore the garb of a sanyasin and travelled to religious places, preaching patriotism.

In the Belur *Math*, where he stayed with his gurubhais after the death of Swami Ramakrishna, along with lessons on spiritualism, Vivekananda used to deliver lectures on French Revolution, the American War of Independence, and Indian History. He used to cry out, "Let Man-Making" be the goal of our life. Let us make this our only sadhna! Away with vain learning!"[10] This makes it clear that his yearning for freedom of the country continued and he looked for ways to give it

> Let Man-Making be the goal of our life. Let us make this our only sadhna! Away with vain learning!

7. See for detail S.N. Banerjea, '*A Nation in the Making*'.
8. Sibanarayan Roy, *Studies in the Bengal Renaissance* Minerva Associates, Calcutta, 2000, p-212.
9. S.N. Banerjea, A *Nation in the Making* p-32.
10. *Life of Swami Vivekananda*, by Eastern & Western Disciples Advaita Ashram, Vol-II, 1913, p-22-28.

practical shape. His brother Bhupendranath Datta, in his book, 'Vivekananda—Prophet-Patriot' writes about young Vivekananda:

"Very few people knew that he (Vivekananda) had revolutionary ideas in the beginning. He wanted to free the country from the foreign yoke. But he failed in this attempt, and seeing the cause of his failure, he tried a different remedy and deflected his attention to another channel. The key to the new venue of his work for India lay there."[11]

His work of regeneration of his motherland started with his travels. He left the *Math* and did not disclose his plans to his gurubhais just told them that he wanted to be alone. On July 15, 1890, he wrote to Swami Sadananda, 'I have my own plans for the future, and they shall be a secret.'[12] From February 1891 onwards he was rarely in touch with them. Mostly by himself he roamed all over the country. He travelled with assumed names and did not reveal his identity to many. By visiting different places, he wanted to know the pulse of the nation and to explore the possibility of an armed revolution as he later revealed. In this connection he met and made friends with Maharaja of Khetri—Ajit Singh, Raja of Baroda–Gaekwar, Raja of Ramnad, Mysore, Kolahpur, Bhavnagar, Hyderabad, Travancore etc. He met the common masses and closely observed the state in which the country had passed into under the colonial rule.

Wherever he stayed during his travels, his patriotic fervour and his concern for the suffering countrymen surpassed his religiosity. In 1888 at Hathras, Vivekananda met a bengali, named Sharat Chandra Gupta, who became his disciple. Sharat was an assistant station-master at Hathras Railway Station. He was so influenced by Vivekananda that he gave up his job and became his disciple. Vivekananda stayed at Sharat's house for a few days and disclosed to him as: "I have a

---

11. Bhupendranath Datta, Swami Vivekananda—Patriot and Prophet, Navabharat Press Calcutta, 1954, p-VIII.

12. *Life*. Vol-I, 1979, p-535.

great mission to fulfil and I am in despair at the smallness of my capacity...This is nothing than the regeneration of my motherland."[13]

At Varanasi, he reminded his young listeners, which included Kelkar, a well-known patriot, their duty towards their motherland. According to Kelkar, the Swami spoke on the topic of India and her distress along with politics, social-reforms and many other issues. Expressing his anguish and anger, he said:

"What is the good of India living in this degeneration and extreme poverty any longer? Every moment she is suffering a hell; no food and no clothes; dishonour and distress is her only lot; she breathes—that is all the sign of life she has got. It is a veritable hellish fire in which she is being consumed slowly and certainly. Was it not far better that she was extinct from the face of the earth."[14]

During his stay at Varanasi, Pramdadas Babu, became his close friend. while taking leave from him Vivekananda told him: "When I shall return here next time I shall burst upon society like a bombshell."[15] How it was going to happen, he did not explain, yet it reveals that he had some plan in his mind.

In 1891, in Alwar at Diwanji's house, Vivekananda exhorted the people in the following words:

"Be strong! Be manly! I have respect even for a wicked person so long as he is manly and strong, for his strength will make him some day give up his wickedness and even renounce all work for selfish ends and will thus eventually bring him to truth."[16]

Haripada Mitra, at whose place Vivekananda stayed in 1892, at Belgaum, wrote: "I had never found in anybody such an intense patriotism. One evening reading in a newspaper that a man had died in Calcutta from starvation, the Swami was overcome with sorrow

I have a great mission to fulfil and I am in despair at the smallness of my capacity...This is nothing than the regeneration of my motherland.

Be strong! Be manly! I have respect even for a wicked person so long as he is manly and strong, for his strength will make him some day give up his wickedness and even renounce all work for selfish ends and will thus eventually bring him to truth.

---

13. Ibid., p-221.
14. *Reminiscences of Vivekananda*, p-403.
15. *Life*, Vol-I, p-248.
16. Ibid., p-271.

and repeated again and again, 'Oh my country! Oh my country!"[17]

Babu Mathura Nath Sinha, a pleader of Bhagalpur, who knew Vivekananda since school days, noted latter's intense patriotism when Vivekananda arrived and lectured at Bhagalpur:

"I discovered that the soul of his teaching was an intense and unselfish patriotism with which he invested and vivified his subjects."[18]

After Bhagalpur, Vivekananda went to Deogarh and there he visited the house of Babu Rajnarain Bose, a noted social reformer and a revolutionary. Grandfather of Aurobindo Ghose, Bose had been Headmaster of the Midnapur government school and had founded the society for the promotion of national feeling among the educated natives of Bengal. Bose did not believe in the constitutional methods for the attainment of freedom, stood for force and advocated formation of secret societies and himself had founded one. Vivekananda had a long talk with him. Though there is no record of their conversation yet the meeting itself is significant as the two were against the policy of mendicancy for the liberation of motherland.

At Madras, he met Ala Singa, a young brahmin teaching Philosophy in a college. Ala Singa was so impressed by Vivekananda that he became his life-long disciple and co-worker in the service of motherland and its people. Ala Singa was a patriot and had close contact with Tilak and other radical leaders of the country. He had formed student groups where political issues were discussed. He arranged Vivekananda's lectures in schools and colleges. Vivekananda's patriotic exhortations covered with religious terminology highly enthused the students and many of them joined the struggle for their country's freedom.[19]

17. Ibid., p-314.
18. Ibid., p-193.
19. C.S. Subramanyam, *MPT Acharya*, Institute of South Indian Studies, Madras, 1995, p-8.

KS Ramaswami Sastri, at whose residence, Vivekananda stayed for nine-days in 1892, later reminisced:

"Practical patriotism means not a mere sentiment or even emotion of love of the motherland but a passion to serve our fellow-countrymen. I have gone all over India on foot and have seen with my own eyes, the ignorance, misery and squalor of our people. My whole soul is afire and I am burning with a fierce desire to change such evil conditions."[20]

K Vyasa Rao, who regularly attended Vivekananda' lectures wrote about Vivekananda's impact on the youth of Madras:

"But everything apart, what endeared him to all was the unalloyed fervour of his patriotism. The youngman, who had renounced all worldly ties and freed himself from bondage, had but one love, his country and one grief, its downfall."[21]

He wrote further that Vivekananda 'bewailed and denounced in unmeasured terms the imbecility of our youngmen'and 'His words flashed as lightening and cut as steel'[22]

Vivekananda's conversations and addresses leave no doubt that he was on a mission and that mission was none other than to rescue his motherland from the foreign yoke. Most of the times, he travelled on foot and many a times, he did not get food or shelter but all these did not diminish his intense love for his motherland. He said:

"...I stand in awe before the unbroken procession of scores of centuries, with here and there a dim link in the chain, only to flare up with added brilliance in the next, and there she is walking with her own majestic steps— my motherland—to fulfil her glorious destiny, which no power on earth or in heaven can check.[23]

> Practical patriotism means not a mere sentiment or even emotion of love of the motherland but a passion to serve our fellow-countrymen. I have gone all over India on foot and have seen with my own eyes, the ignorance, misery and squalor of our people. My whole soul is afire and I am burning with a fierce desire to change such evil conditions.

> ...I stand in awe before the unbroken procession of scores of centuries, with here and there a dim link in the chain, only to flare up with added brilliance in the next, and there she is walking with her own majestic steps—my motherland—to fulfil her glorious destiny, which no power on earth or in heaven can check.

20. *Reminiscences of Vivekananda*. p-100.
21. *Life* Vol-I, p-368. 1979.
22. Ibid.,
23. C.W. Vol-IV, p-260. 1947.

...My life's allegiance is to my motherland, and if I had a thousand lives, every moment of the whole series would be consecrated to your service, my countrymen."[24]

Euologising India wherein wisdom, prosperity and spirituality ushered first, Vivekananda said:

"This is the ancient land where wisdom made its home before it went into any other country, the same India whose influx of spirituality is represented, as it were, on the material plane, by rolling rivers like oceans, where the eternal Himalayas, rising tier above tier with their snow caps, look as it were, into the very mysteries of heaven. Here is the same India whose soil has been trodden by the feet of the great sages that ever lived. Here first sprang up inquiries into the nature of man, and into the internal world. Here first arose the doctrines of immortality of the soul, the existence of the Supervising God, an immanent God in nature and man, and here the highest ideals of religion and philosophy have attained their culminating points. This is the land from whence, like tidal waves, spirituality and philosophy have again and again rushed out and deluged the whole world, and this is the land from whence once more such tides must proceed in order to bring life and vigor into the decaying races of mankind. It is the same India, which has withstood the shocks of centuries, of hundreds of foreign invasions, of hundreds of upheavals of manners and customs. It is the same land, which stands firmer than any rock in the world, with its undying vigour, indestructible life. Its life is of the nature of the soul, without beginning and without end, immortal; and we are the children of such a country."[25]

In one of his lectures Vivekananda explained that how many countries of the world owed their riches to the Indian commerce:

24. C.W. Vol-IV, p-258. 1947.
25. C.W. Vol-III, 1948, p-285.

"Of all the causes which have worked for the present state of human civilization from the ancient times, the commerce of India is perhaps the most important. From time immemorial, India has beaten all other countries in point of fertility and commercial industries. Up till a century ago, the whole of the world's demand for cotton cloth, jute, indigo, lac, rice, diamonds and pearls used to be supplied from India. No other country could produce such excellent silk and woolen fabrics, like kincop, etc. as India. Again India has been the land of various spices as cloves, cardamom, pepper, nutmeg, mace etc. Most people are ignorant of the extent to which the opulence of ancient countries like Babylon, Persia, Greece and Rome owed to Indian commerce. After the downfall of Rome, Baghdad, and Venice, Genoa became the chief marts of Indian commerce. When the Turks closed the trade routes to India for the Italians, Columbus, a Genoese, tried to explore a new route to India. When the Portuguese discovered a new route to India doubling Africa, the fortune of India smiled upon Portugal; then came the turn of French, the Dutch, the Danes and the English."[26]

Vivekananda's vast knowledge which he had acquired during his college days by reading numerous books other than the prescribed texts, and his sharp intellect easily detected the real motive of the rulers for enslaving India. He stated that British rule in India was neither divinely ordained nor a blessing. Here he differed with Brahmoes as well as the moderate Congress leaders. He explained to the people that the real motive of India's enslavement by the British was economic.

"The conquest of India by England is not a conquest of Jesus or Bible as we are often asked to believe...Behind the name of the Lord Jesus, the Bible...there is always the virtual presence of

The conquest of India by England is not a conquest of Jesus or Bible as we are often asked to believe...Behind the name of the Lord Jesus, the Bible...there is always the virtual presence of England—that England whose warflag is the factory chimney whose troops are the merchantmen, whose battlefields are the market-places of the world and whose Empress is the shining Goddess of Fortune herself.

26. D.V. Athalye, *Swami Vivekananda, The Patriot-Saint* Pub-Ashish, N.D. 1979, p-218.

England—that England whose warflag is the factory chimney whose troops are the merchantmen, whose battlefields are the market—places of the world and whose Empress is the shining Goddess of Fortune herself."[27]

He was well-aware of the drainage of Indian wealth to Britain and the damage it was causing to Indian economy. Rebuking his countrymen for bearing the foreign domination, he stated:

"Foreigners use India's raw-material to make gold, and you are just carrying their burden like donkeys. Foreigners become richer and richer by taking primary goods from India and processing them by their intelligence and you people have locked up your intelligence in a chest and are crying for bread after allowing others to take your own wealth. 'Trampled under other's feet, doing slavery for others, are you men or more? You are not worth a pin's head! In this fertile country with abundant water supply, where Nature produces wealth and harvest a thousand times more than in others, you have no food for your stomach, no clothes to cover your body! In this country of abundance, the produce of which has been the cause of the spread of civilization in other countries, you are reduced to such straits! Your condition is worse than that of a dog. And you glory in your Vedas and Vedanta! A nation that cannot provide for its simple food and clothing, which always depends on others for its subsistence—what is there for it to vaunt about? Throw your religious observances overboard for the present and be first prepared for the struggle of existence."[28]

Continously one finds anger and anguish in his outpour against the British.

"...they (English) have their heels on our necks, they have sucked the last drop of our blood for their pleasures, they have carried away with them millions of

> ...they (English) have their heels on our necks, they have sucked the last drop of our blood for their pleasures, they have carried away with them millions of our money, while our people have starved in villages and provinces.

27. C.W. Vol-IV, 1947, p-385.
28. C.W. Vol-VII, 1947, p-142-143.

our money, while our people have starved in villages and provinces.[29]

They ground down poor people for their own wealth. They heard not the voice of distress. They ate from gold and silver, when the Indians cried for bread.[30]

For seven years he had made efforts to rouse his countrymen. He knew about the secret revolutionary organisations in Italy and France and the manufacturing of arms by such societies. Vivekananda too established contacts with a gun-maker Hiram Maxim. However, he did not get response from the country. He revealed later about this to Sister Christine:

"I had the idea of forming a combination of Indian Princes for the overthrow of the foreign yoke. For this reason, from the Himalayans to Cape-Comorine I have travelled all over the country. For that reason, I made friends with the gun-maker Sir Hiram Maxim. But I got no response from the country."[31]

Vivekanand's failure to move the notables and the commoners did not diminish his urge for freedom. He continued his efforts by adopting a different way. He decided to visit America not for religious purpose but for the fulfillment of the mission he had set before himself.

"I did not go to America, as most of you know, for the Parliament of Religions, but this demon of a feeling was in me and within my soul. I travelled twelve years all over India. Finding no way to work for my countrymen and that is why I went to America. Most of you know that, who knew me then. Who cared for this Parliament of Religions? Here was my own flesh and blood sinking every day; and who cared for them? This was my first step."[32]

---

29. Ibid.,
30. Ibid., p-279.
31. Datta, p-IX.
32. *Lectures From Colombo to Almora*, p-138.

He definitely had some plan in his mind. It is evident from his letter written to Ala Singa on May 28, 1894 from US:

"Act on the educated youngmen, bring them together, and organize them. Great things can be done by great sacrifices only. No selfishness, no name , no fame; yours or mine,...work the idea, the plan... to the wheel put your shoulders! Stop not to look back...Remember 'The grass when made into rope by being joined together can even chain a mad elephant."[33]

While in America, he visited places connected with the war of independence and the civil war. He admired Washington, the leader of the war of independence and Abraham Lincon, who abolished slavery in America and called them 'true Karamyogis'. However in the land of liberty he also felt humiliations and discriminations and encountered a strong racial prejudice for being from the subject nation, which created many hardships for him in his public and in his private life. No hair saloon was ready to cut his hair and none in the restaurant was willing to serve him meals.[34] In New York among other things, it was extremely difficult for him to secure a proper lodging. Landladies invariably assured him that they had no feeling themselves, but they were afraid they would lose their borders or lodgers if they took an Asiatic into their house. This forced Vivekananda to accept dingy lodgings. At Boston he was hooted because of his red coat and turban. A great number of men and boys followed him in the busy part of the town and teased him. Vivekananda had to hide in a dark place to save himself. This uncivilized behaviour in a civilized country made him cry for his country. The stigma of slavery had to be wiped off for getting equal treatment. He poured out his feelings in his famous poem '*Song of the Sanyasins*' composed at the Thousand Island Park in July 1895, which became a religious sermon for all the patriots.

---

33. *Life*. Vol-I 1979, p-551.
34. C.W. Vol-V, 1947, p-302.

"Strike off thy fetters! Bonds that bind thee down,
Of shinning gold, or darker, baser are,
Love, hate-good, bad-and all the dual throng.
Know slave is slave, caressed or whipped, not free,
For fetters though of gold, are not less strong to bind;
Then, off with them, Sanyasin bold! Say-
                              Om Tat Sat, Om,!
Where seekest thou? That freedom, friend this world
Nor that, can give, In books and temple vain
They search. Thine only is the hand that holds
The rope that drags thee on, then cease lament,
Let go thy hold, Sqnyasin bold! Say-
                              Om Tat Sat, Om!"[35]

In America, Vivekananda did not speak on religion only. He also spoke on Indian art, culture, customs, prosperity and heritage of harmony of the pre-colonial rule period. Brooklyn Standard Union quoted excerpts from his lecture on February 27, 1895 wherin he spoke not only about the beauty of his native land but also its contribution to the world. He proudly proclaimed:

"India has given to antiquity the earliest scientifical physicians... she has even contributed to modern medical science by the discovery of various chemicals and by teaching you how to reform misshapen ears and noses. Even more it has done in mathematics, for algebra, geometry, astronomy, and the triumph of modern science—mixed mathematics—were all invented in India, just so much as the ten numerals, the very cornerstone of all present civilization, were discovered in India....In manufacture, India was the first to make cotton and purple (dye), it was proficient in all works of jewellry and the very word 'sugar' as well as the article itself, is the product of India. Lastly, she has invented the game of the chess and the cards and the dice. So great, in fact was the superiority of India in

---

35. C.W. Vol-IV, 1948, p-329.

every respect, that it drew to her borders the hungry cohorts of Europe, and therby indirectly brought about the discovery of America."[36]

American audience was amazed to hear such utterances from a monk. Even his religious addresses and lectures contained his patriotic fervour. He could not tolerate disrespect shown to his country and shot back whenever critical remarks were hurled against anything related with India. He had the courage to express his views. In one of his lectures, Vivekanand said:

"One thing I must tell you....To come over to my own country and abuse all my forefathers, my religion and everything... If all India stands up and takes all the mud that is at the bottom of the Indian Ocean and throws it up against the western countries; it will not be doing an infinitesimal part of that which you are doing to us."[37]

At Annisquam, a village in Boston, Vivekananda spoke with anger and bitterness about the British tyranny in India. He denounced the British rule in India and exploitation of its people. A notable feature of Vivekananda's addresses at this time, which the newspapers did not fail to notice, was his patriotism. To quote from one of these:

"His patriotism was perfervid. The manner in which he speaks of 'my country' is most touching. That one phrase revealed him not as a monk, but as a man of his people."[38]

He refuted European's claim that their rule over subjugated countries was for the betterment of the people of those lands.

"And I ask you Europeans, what country you have ever raised to better condition? Wherever you have found weaker races, you have exterminated them by the roots as it were. You settled down on their lands and

> One thing I must tell you....To come over to my own country and abuse all my forefathers, my religion and everything... If all India stands up and takes all the mud that is at the bottom of the Indian Ocean and throws it up against the western countries; it will not be doing an infinitesimal part of that which you are doing to us.

36. C.W. Vol-II, p-511-512. 1970.
37. *Life* Vol-I 1979, p-462.
38. Ibid., p-457.

they are gone for ever. What is the history of your America, your Australia and New Zealand, your pacific islands and South Africa? Where are those aboriginal races there today? They are all exterminated, you have killed them outright, as if they were wild beasts. It is only where you have not the power to do so, and there only, that these nations are still alive."[39]

No wonder, he was taken as a political delegate rather than a religious delegate by many Americans.

He came to United Kingdom from America and even there, the cause of his country was uppermost in his addresses and lectures. Like his mentors and predecessors i.e., Raja Rammohun Roy and Keshab Chandra Sen who had represented Indian interest in London, Vivekananda too spoke for his country. But unlike them Vivekananda was a sanyasin and he was aware of this constraint but the love and concern of his country could not stop him from criticizing the colonial rulers. In London, while speaking at the Cambridge gathering, Vivekananda pointed out how India lost its prosperity and suffered under the British rule.

"They (English) are rulers and merchants as well. Mere revenue does not suffice their requirement; they also claim all the profits from business. They want the revenue from all the posts and they want also all the profits made out of commerce, trade and manufactures."[40] In the same address he also stated that India had been disarmed as never done before.[41]

At another place, he pointed out about what Britain has given to in comparison to previous regimes under Hindus and Muslims.

"India has been conquered again and again for years and last and worst of came the Englishman. You look about India, what has the Hindu left? Wonderful temples everywhere. What has Mohammedan left?

India has been conqured again and again for years and last and worst of came the Englishman. You look about India, what has the Hindu left? Wonderful temples everywhere. What has Mohammedan left? Beautiful palaces. What has the Englishmen left? Nothing but mounds of brandy bottles!

39. See Vivekananda's Lectur 'East & West' in detail.
40. *Vivekananda in Indian Newspapers*, p-314.
41. Ibid.,

Beautiful palaces. What has the Englishmen left? Nothing but mounds of brandy bottles!"[42]

No wonder an Englishman remarked that Vivekananda seemed more like a warrior than a priest."[43]

During his stay in the west, he closely observed the functioning of the political system. The representative political institutions and rights being enjoyed by the people made him lament their absence in his own homeland. In a letter written to Miss Mary on the 20th September 1893 from US, Vivekanand unmasked the British rule categorically stating that the main idea on which the British in India was based was the 'blood sucking'. He wrote:

"For writing a few words of innocent criticism men are being hurried to transportation for life, others imprisoned without trial; and nobody knows when his head will be off... This is the state of things—even education will no more be permitted to spread; freedom of press stopped already,(of course we have been disarmed) the bit of the self government granted to them for some years is being quickly taken off. We are watching what next!

There has been a reign of terror in India for some years. English soldiers are killing our men and outraging our women—only to be sent home with passage and pension at our expense. We are in terrible gloom....Mary you can afford to be optimistic can I? Suppose you publish this letter—the law just passed in India, will allow the English Government of India to drag me from here to India and kill me without trial."[44]

However in United Kingdom, he got his most devoted disciple Margaret Noble whom he named Nivedita. She was an Irish woman. Her grandfather was a freedom fighter and had struggled for the independence of Ireland but her father had a religious bent of

42. Letters p-98.
43. Manmohan Ganguly, *Swami Vivekananda, A Study* Contemporary Pub. Calcutta, 1907, p-64.
44. C.W. Vol-VIII, 1959, p-476.

mind. Nivedita had both traits in her. Like Vivekananda, she too was young, cosmopolitan and rational in outlook, had the quest to know the religious truths, hated domination and was compassionate towards the downtrodden. She was also in touch with the well-known political revolutionaries and philosophers of Europe. In London she was attracted to Free Ireland, an Irish revolutionary organization. She became a member of the organization and spoke and organized cells in South England. Her meeting with Vivekananda gave a new turn to her life and earned her a special place in the Indian history. She regularly attended Vivekanandas's lectures and accepted him as her spiritual Master.

In London Vivekananda's longing for his country increased with each passing day. "I loved India before I came away; now the very dust of India has become holy to me,"[45] he remarked one day. Sister Nivedita, who closely observed him during his stay in London, said: "There was one thing deep in Master's nature, that he never knew how to adjust. This was the love of his country and his resentment of her sufferings."[46]

> There was one thing deep in Master's nature, that he never knew how to adjust. This was the love of his country and his resentment of her sufferings.

His lectures won him recognition, respect and even reverence in foreign countries however his patriotic urge and aspiration made him restless for his motherland. He decided to return to India and awaken his countrymen. On his arrival in Madras, he gave a clarion call to the people to rise for the regeneration of the motherland. He said that one should consider it a great honour, if one had to go through hell in doing good for the country. He gave four lectures in Madras. The two lectures 'My Plan of Campaign' and 'The Future of India' were like political sermons. In his lecture, 'The Future of India', he emphasized the need for unity among all Indians and said that Indians lacked unity and fellow-feeling, the secrets of national

---

45. C.W. Vol-III, 1948, p-309.
46. Sister Nivedita, *The Master. As I Saw Him.*. p-50.

greatness. He pointed out that disunion and jealousy of each other have been the greatest defects in the national life. Here are his denunciations "We cannot combine, we do not love each other; we are intensely selfish, not three of us can come together without hating each other, without being jealous of each other."[47] His lectures made people, particularly the youth filled with patriotic zeal.

However, his concept of patriotism was different from the prevalent one. Motherland should be taken not just as a country but as a Goddess and duty towards the country should be like worship. He said:

> For the next fifty years this alone shall be our keynote—this our great Mother India. Let all other vain Gods disappear for that time from our minds.[48]

Secondly a true patriot must have the will to surmount mountain-high obstructions, even if the world stood against him, he must proceed steadily towards his own goal.[49]

Thirdly, a patriot should feel from the heart and be concerned with the plight of his people and dedicate himself to his country." In his lecture on 'My Plan of Campaign' he explained to a huge crowd:

> "I believe in patriotism, and also I have my own ideal of patriotism. Three things are necessary for great achievements. First feel from the heart. What is in the intellect or reason? It goes a few steps and there it stops. But through the heart comes inspiration...Feel therefore, my would be reformers, my would be patriots! Do you feel that millions and millions of the descendants have become next door neighbours to brutes. Do you feel that millions are starving today and millions have been starving for ages? Do you feel that ignorance has come over the land as a dark cloud. Does

For the next fifty years this alone shall be our keynote—this our great Mother India. Let all other vain Gods disappear for that time from our minds.

---

47. R.C. Majumdar, *Swami Vivekananda: A Historical View*, General Pub & Printer, Calcutta, 1965, p-121.
48. C.W. Vol-III, 1948, p-309.
49. Lizelle Reymond, *The Dedicated-Biography of Nivedita* The John Day Company, New York, 1953, p-128.

it make you restless? Does it make you sleepless? Has it gone into your blood, coursing through your veins becoming consonant with your heart beats? Has it made you almost mad? Are you seized with that idea of the misery of ruin, and have you forgotten all your name, your fame, your wives your children, your property, even your bodies? Have you done that? That is the first step to become a patriot, the very first step."[50]

The above definition of patriotism given by Vivekanand sharply differed from the one represented by the Indian National Congress. To Vivekananda it meant supreme sacrifice, devotion and dedication. He did not believe in meager political reforms through constitutional means—petitioning, pleasing and pleading the British rulers.

"That is not the way to build up patriotism anywhere. Beggars bowl has no place in a Baniks (Merchant's) world of machine, mammon and merchandise.[51] With this mere echoing of others, with this base imitation of others, with this dependence of others, this slavish weakness...will you attain by means of your disgraceful cowardice the freedom deserved only by the brave and heroic."[52]

The moderate congressmen were keen to secure the cooperation of the colonial rulers for the socio-economic and political development of the country. Vivekananda differed with their approach. He discounted the efforts of the moderates by saying "all progress at the dictation of another whose hand is at India's throat, is valueless"[53]

The Indian National Congress in his opinion was neither representing nor working for the masses. It was keen only in grabbing political power and replacing the English by themselves. Attacking the narrow attitude of the Congress, he said:

---

50. C.W. Vol-III, 1948, p-226.
51. Datta, p-332
52. C.W. Vol-IV, 1948, p-412-413.
53. See Vivekananda's Lectures on India and Her Problems.

Our young fools
organise meetings
to get more power
from the English.
They only laugh.
None deserves
liberty who is not
ready to give
liberty. Suppose the
English give over to
you all the power,
why the powers
that be then, will
hold the people
down, and let them
not have it. Slaves
want power to
make slaves.

"Our young fools organise meetings to get more power from the English. They only laugh. None deserves liberty who is not ready to give liberty. Suppose the English give over to you all the power, why the powers that be then, will hold the people down, and let them not have it. Slaves want power to make slaves."[54]

Criticising the congress leaders as not true patriots, Vivekananda thundered:

"Who thinks of raising these sunken downtrodden millions? A few thousand graduates do not make a nation. True our opportunities are fewer, but still there are enough to feed and clothe and make three hundred millions more comfortable...Ninety per cent of our people are without education—who thinks of that? These Babus, the so called patriots."[55]

He was conscious of the fact that freedom would not end India's troubles, it would be only a first step towards regeneration, demanding the services of the patriots more keenly. "Suppose the Government gives all you need, where are the men able to keep up things demanded? So make men first."[56]

In a passionately patriotic outburst, he stated:

"O Bharat, wilt thou rely up on this institution of the others, this mimicry, this anxiety to win others approbation, this imbecile slavishness, this hateful abominable hard-heartedness to win high authority? Wilt thou, with the aid of shameful cowardice, achieve independence...? Do not forget, your society is the veriest shadow of the great illusion, do not forget the lowly, the poor, the ignorant, the currier, the sweeper are your blood, are your brethren. O, ye brave one, take courage, be proud that you are an Indian, and proudly proclaim I am an Indian, every Indian is my brother...The soil of India is my highest heaven. India's

54. C.W. Vol-IV, 1948, p-313.
55. Letters, p-1350.
56. Datta, p-402.

good is my good."[57] When asked whether he had faith in what Congress was doing, He said:

"No I have no faith. But, of course, something is better than nothing and it is good to push the sleeping nation from all sides to wake it up. Can you tell me what Congress has been doing for the masses? Do you think merely passing a few resolutions will bring you freedom? I have no faith in that. The masses must be awakened first. Let them have full meals, and they will work out their own salvation. If Congress does any thing for them, it has my sympathy."[58]

In 1897, a famine engulfed Bengal and took a heavy toll of human life. Vivekananda, castigated the Congress for doing nothing for the sufferers. In a letter to his brother disciple Alakhananda, he wrote, "In these days of mire famine, food disease and pestilence, tell me where your Congressmen are. Will it do merely to say, 'Hand the Government of the country to us?"[59]

Vivekananda's patriotic preaching and his ideal of future India inspired nationalists of all shades. They sought his advice and guidance in the struggle for India's freedom. In the end of the year 1901 Indian National Congress's session was held in Calcutta. Many influential leaders of the Congress including Mahatma Gandhi visited Belur. During the evening many delegates used to gather at his place and discuss at length the problems. One day one of the political leaders remarked that he had behind him "all the Mahrattas" while another leader said he had "all the Bengalis" but "where are the masses?" asked Vivekananda. He expressed his unhappiness as the Congress was not doing anything for the elevation of the masses.[60] An editor of a paper called 'The Advocate' published from Lucknow, was in Calcutta to cover the

> In these days of mire famine, food disease and pestilence, tell me where your Congressmen are. Will it do merely to say, 'Hand the Government of the country to us?

---

57. C.W. Vol-IV, p-412-413.
58. Life. Vol-II, p-698.
59. C.W. Vol-VI, 1956, p-426.
60. Reymond, p-242.

Congress proceedings, he met the Swami and later wrote:

"When we last saw him in Calcutta, during the Congress session, he was eloquently talking, in pure and chaste hindi...about schemes for the regeneration of India, his face beaming with enthusiasm."[61]

Despite a critic of elitistic approach and attitude of the Congress towards the socio-economic and political issues, Vivekananda appreciated its secular character. When asked whether he had given any attention to the Congress movement, he answered:

"I do not claim to have given much, my work is in another part of the field. But I regard the movement as significant and heartily wish it success. A nation is being made out of India's different races. It will certainly lead in the working out India's homogeneity in her acquiring what we may call democratic ideas."[62]

Politically, he was closer to Congress's militants and revolutionaries and had contacts with some of their leaders. Once while going from Bombay to Poona, Vivekanand and Tilak travelled together in the same train and compartment. Vivekananda stayed in Tilak's house for a week. Though nothing is known about their conversations yet the stay itself is a significant proof that the two were like minded as far as the freedom of the country was concerned. In 1902, on his Calcutla visit, Tilak also visited the Belur *Math* to meet the swami. According to Tilak, in their conversation Vivekananda remarked that both should change their role. Tilak should work in Bengal while he would take over his work in Maharashtra.[63]

The huge following of Vivekananda, particularly of youngsters, made the authorities suspicious of his moves and motives. Vivekananda's activities were watched and

> I do not claim to have given much, my work is in another part of the field. But I regard the movement as significant and heartily wish it success. A nation is being made out of India's different races. It will certainly lead in the working out India's homogeneity in her acquiring what we may call democratic ideas.

61. *Last Days of Swami Vivekananda* by Eastern & Western Disciples, Advaita, Ashram Calcutta, 1927, p-36.
62. C.W. Vol-VI, 1956, p-128, Datta, p-129.
63. *Reminiscences of Swami Vivekananda*, p-10.

his letters were opened by the post offices. The Office of the Director, Criminal Intelligence wrote a note when the latter was touring through the various states in Kathiawar that his religious lectures did not exercise much influence on his hearers, but it was noticed that he took an interest in politics. The Government was so scared of the impact of his teachings that it denied permission to Maharaja of Kashmir who wished to hand over to Swami an estate on which a sanskrit college was to be established.[64]

They kept a close watch on his activities. Once, when Vivekananda was living in Calcutta with his disciples, a police officer who was also a friend of the family, invited him for dinner. Instead of serving dinner the officer spoke about other matters until suddenly lowering his voice he said, "come now, you had better make a clean breast of it and tell me the truth. You know you cannot fool me with your stories for I know your game. You and your gang pretend to be religious men, but I have positive information that you are conspiring against the government.' 'What do you mean?' asked Vivekananda. 'What conspiracies you are speaking of, and what have we to do with them?'. 'That is what I want to know,' coolly replied the officer. 'I am convinced it is some nefarious plot, and you are the ringleader. Out with the whole truth, and then I shall arrange that you are made an approver.' 'If you know everything, why don't you come and arrest us and search our house.?" Said Vivekananda, and rising he quietly closed the door. Vivekananda was an athletic young man of powerful build, while the police officer was a puny, wizened creature. Turning round Vivekananda said. 'You have called me to your house on a false pretext and have made a false accusation against me and my companions. That is your profession. I, on the other hand, have been taught not to resent an insult. If I had been a criminal and a conspirator, there would be nothing to prevent me from ringing your neck before you could call out for

64. Reymond, p-120.

help. As it is I leave you in peace.' And Vivekananda opened the door and went out, leaving the redoubtable police officer speechless with ill-concealed fright."[65]

The spies followed wherever he went. Sister Nivedita, who accompanied the Swami to Almora, wrote about it to Mrs. Hammond on May 22, 1898:

"You cannot imagine what race hatred means, living in England. Manliness seems a barrier to nothing. One of the monks has had a warning this morning that the police are watching the Swami through the spies. The Swami laughs at it, though I cannot help attaching some importance to it. The Government would be made to attempt to interfere with him, for it would rouse a country and I the most loyal English woman who ever breathed in this country (I could not have suspected the depth of my loyalty till I got here), would be the first to rise up."[66]

Initially, even Raja of Ramnad doubted the bonafides of Vivekananda and refused to give the promised rupees 10,000 for the Swami's United States visit. The Raja 'suspected that the Swami, being a Bengali, and an educated one too, might indulge in politics and scheming to his (Raja's) deteriment'[67]

Raja was one among numerous who discern Swami's passionate patriotism in his preachings. Vivekananda knew it and that is why he publicly denied having political connection with any organisation. "I am no politician or political agitator. I care only for the spirit....So must warn the Calcutta people that no political significance be ever attached falsely to any of my writings or sayings."[68]

Without involving himself directly in active politics, Vivekanand contributed greatly in designing the destiny of Modern India. Through the religious

65. Reminiscences, p-21, *Life*-Vol-I, p-307.
66. Pravrajika, *Sister Nivedita*, p-59.
67. *Life*, Vol-I, p-373.
68. *Life*, Vol-II, p-337, Reymond, p-119.

medium he kept on working towards making the people politically, aware and assertive. He even criticised the Brahmo Samaj and the Arya Samaj and other sects as "useless mixtures...voices of apology to... English masters."[69]

He devised new ways and new principles for achieving the desired goals. He asked the people to shed ignorance; to shed divisions based on caste, region or religion; to shed all sorts of weaknesses; to look forward; to be fearless and to develop international outlook.

"A nation of dyspeptics indulging in antics to the accompaniment of khol and kartal and singing kirtans and other songs of sentimental type... I wish to stimulate energy, even by means of martial music, and proscribe everything that titillates languorous sentiments."[70]

He spoke to his disciple Sharat Chandra Chakravarti:

"Is it not any wonder that hearing day and night from boyhood these soft and sentimental songs and music, the nation is becoming more and more effeminate? What degradation can be more complete? Where are your dhhak, dhhole, turi bheri and singa, your drums, kettledrums, tom-toms, trumpets and horns gone? Let the children and youngmen hear their deep solemn austere and rousing notes. We have to sound the damaru and horn; we must produce on drums symphonies that are martial and heroic like that of Brahma Rudra Tal. We must shake the earth...We must stop for the present those songs and music which stimulate the softer feelings in men and, instead, make them hear and cultivate those in Dhrupad and the like...In all our sphere of activity we should display the austere loftiness of spirit which heroism breathes. In following such an ideal of manliness alone there is the welfare of Motherland."[71]

A nation of dyspeptics indulging in antics to the accompaniment of khol and kartal and singing kirtans and other songs of sentimental type... I wish to stimulate energy, even by means of martial music, and proscribe everything that titillates languorous sentiments.

69. Amiya Sen, p-327.
70. C.W. Vol-VII, 1947, p-230.
71. *Last Days of Swami Vivekananda*, p-43.

He asked people to stop looking up to God for help. Instead they should help themselves.

"What can meditation do? What can the mantra and Tantra do? You must stand on your own feet. You must have this new method—the method of man-making. The true man is he who is strong as strength itself."[72]

Admonishing all Indians for the deplorable situation of the country, he said:

"Can that be called society which is formed by an aggregate of men who are like lumps of clay, like lifeless machines, like heaped up pebbles? How can such society fare-well?"[73]

It was cowardness and inactivity on the part of the people, which was responsible for the then state of the country. "You have well-nigh thrown the country into ruin by crying, 'It is impossible, it is impossible! What cannot human effort achieve?"[74]

Once when Nivedita told him about her inability to devote time for meditation, Vivekananda remarked "Never complain of not having enough time for prayer and meditation", "your mission and your achievement lie in your work…My mission is not Ramakrishna's nor Vedanta's nor anything but simply to bring manhood to this people."[75]

The Swami emphasized on strength which was essential for gaining freedom. His messages covered with religion conveyed political massage and would light the patriotic fire in the hearts of his listeners.

"It is man-making religion that we want. It is man-making theories that we want. It is man-making education all round that we want."[76]

> What can meditation do? What can the mantra and Tantra do? You must stand on your own feet. You must have this new method—the method of man-making. The true man is he who is strong as strength itself.

> Can that be called society which is formed by an aggregate of men who are like lumps of clay, like lifeless machines, like heaped up pebbles? How can such society fare-well?

> It is man-making religion that we want. It is man-making theories that we want. It is man-making education all round that we want.

72. C.W. Vol-III, 1948, p-447.
73. Letters, p-402-403.
74. C.W. Vol-VII, 1947.
75. Reymond, p-153.
76. C.W. Vol-III, 1948, p-447.

He used to tell his listeners that infinite strength itself is religion and God.

"Never lose faith in yourself, you can do anything in the universe, 'Never weaken, all power is yours', 'Every one of you must be a giant', The greatest sin is to think yourself weak...stand up and say, I am the Master, the Master of all. We forge the chain and we alone can break it, and 'Let name and fame and money go; they are terrible bondage. Feel the wonderful atmosphere of freedom.[77]

Even at the gate of the death, in the greatest danger, in the thick of the battlefield, at the bottom of the ocean, on the top of the mountains, in the thickest of the forest, tell yourself 'I am He, I am He'. Day and night say 'I am He'. It is the greatest strength; it is religion.[78]

It is against the big tree that the great winds strike', 'poking a fire makes it burn better', and 'a snake struck on the head raises its hood', 'face the brute, face it boldly".[79]

He prefered Satan like spirit for the cause of the country. No wonder the favourite character of Vivekananda in literature was Milton's Satan. 'The only good man I had any respect for was Satan who thus exhorts his comrades:

"Fallen Cherub, to be weak is miserable,

Doing or suffering."[80]

He used to appreciate Satan even in his religious sermons knowing fully well that Satan revolted against God. He characterized Chengiz Khan, Napoleon and Alexander as great souls and often cited their unmatched spirits against all odds.[81]

> Even at the gate of the death, in the greatest danger, in the thick of the battlefield, at the bottom of the ocean, on the top of the mountains, in the thickest of the forest, tell yourself 'I am He, I am He'. Day and night say 'I am He'. It is the greatest strength; it is religion.

77. C.W. Vol-VII, p-52, 1947.
78. C.W. Vol-III, 1948, p-26.
79. Letters, p-464.
80. Subodh Chandra Sen Gupta, *Swami Vivekananda and Indian Nationalism*, Sahitya Samsad, Calcutta 1984, p-60.
81. *Notes of Some Wandering*, p-74.

He was disappointed by the modern boys and would often deplore saying 'What would these namby-pamby boys, with no strength in the body, no intellect in the brain and no courage in the heart do."[82]

He wanted boys like *Nachiketa*, the hero of *Kathopanishad*, who was a boy full of fire, courage and spirit which remained undaunted and unruffled even when he met the king of death.[83]

> What I want is the muscles of iron and nerves of steel, inside which dwells a mind of the same material as that of the thunderbolt is made. Strength, Manhood, Kshatriya-Virya and Brahma-Teja.

"What I want is the muscles of iron and nerves of steel, inside which dwells a mind of the same material as that of the thunderbolt is made. Strength, Manhood, Kshatriya-Virya and Brahma-Teja.[84]

Have no weakness even in the face of death, and 'he who struggles is better than he who never attempts used to enthuse and arouse everyone.[85] Without freedom life is not worth living hence get freedom at the cost of life. "Conquest is my Mantram" he proclaimed. "There is that human instinct to rebel against nature's law...we are born rebels...No laws for us...As long as we obey the laws we are like machines, and goes the universe...Freedom is the song of the soul.[86]

"It is rebellion against nature, struggle for self preservation, that differentiates spirit from matter. Where there is life there is struggle, there is the manifestation of the spirit. Read the history of all nations, and you will find that that is law. It is only this nation which drifts with nature, and you are more dead than alive. You are in a hypnotized state."[87]

During his visit to Lahore in 1897, he visited four colleges and interacted with students and suggested they serve their motherland with a religious zeal. Speaking before an assembly of the students, he said:

---

82. *Centenary Celebrations*, 1962,-63, p-208
83. Ibid.,
84. Letters, p-34.
85. C.W. Vol-VII, 1947, p-87.
86. C.W. Vol-I, 1947, Rept. 1950, p-334.
87. Life. Vol-I, p-490-91.

'Slaves must become great masters. So give up being slaves.' Immediately, on the spot, the students formed an association as suggested by the Swami.[88]

He gave an inspiring call:

"Love cannot come through fear, its basis is freedom when we really begin to love the world, then we understand what is meant by brotherhood and mankind and not before...Come out in the broad open light of the day, come out from the little narrow paths, for how can the infinite soul rest content to live and die in small holes? Break that chains and be free...Trample law under your feet. There is no law in human nature, there is no destiny, no fate. How can there be law in infinity? Freedom is its watchword. Freedom is its nature, its birthright."[89]

It seems Tilak followed Vivekananda when he gave the slogan 'Swaraj is my birthright and I shall have it'

"The idea of freedom. This is the idea that guides each footsteps of ours, make our movement possible, determine our relation to each other, nay is the very warp and woof in the fabric of human life.[90]

Freedom is the motive of the universe, freedom is its goal.[91]

Everything that we perceive around us is struggling towards the freedom, from the atom to the man, from insentient, lifeless particle of matter to the highest existence on earth, the human soul. The whole universe is in fact the result of this struggle for freedom."[92]

He used to advice his followers to follow Upanishads and Gita as both the scriptures do not talk of salvation but freedom and manliness. He told Sister Nivedita in course of a talk in 1898: "I preach only that one idea—

88. *Vivekananda in Indian Newspapers*, p-607.
89. C.W. Vol-II, 1970, p-323.
90. *Letters*, p-255.
91. C.W. Vol-IV, p-534, 1970, Calcutta.
92. C.W. Vol. V, 1947, p-108.

strength. The quintessence of Vedas and Vedanta and all, lies in that word."[93]

He told his disciples that they must learn to seek death, not life, to hurl oneself upon the sword's point. Vivekananda emphasized over the worship of *Kali*, the symbol of strength. He was critical of Buddhism as it preached non-violence and lacked in power and force. In a poem—*Kali* the Mother, Vivekananda stated the same emotions:

> *For Terror is Thy name*
> *Death is in Thy breath*
> *Who dare misery love*
> *And hug the form of death*
> *Dance in Destruction's dance*
> *To him the Mother comes.*[94]

"Those who are always down-hearted and dispirited in this life can do no work; from life to life they come and go wailing and moaning. 'The earth is enjoyed by heroes'—this is the unfailing truth. Be a hero. Always say, 'I have no fear'. Tell this to everybody-'Have no fear, fear is death, fear is sin, fear is hell, fear is unrighteousness, fear is wrong life."[95]

At another place, he said: "Your country requires heroes, be heroes, stand like a rock...What India wants is a new electric fire to stir up fresh vigor in the national vein. Be brave, be brave, man dies but once."[96]

Exhorting his countrymen to be ready as the freedom was round the corner, he said:

"The longest night seems to be passing away, the sorest trouble seems to be coming to an end at last, the seeming corpse appears to be awakening and a voice is coming to us—away back where history and even

93. *Reminiscences*, p-277.
94. C.W. Vol-IV, 1948, p-319.
95. Ibid. Vol-VII, 1947, p-134.
96. Ibid.,

tradition fails to peep into the gloom of the past,
coming down from there, reflected as it were from peak
to peak of the infinite Himalayas of knowledge, and of
love, and of work, India, this motherland of ours—a
voice is coming unto us, gentle firm and yet
unmistakable in its utterances, and is gaining volume as
days pass by and behold , the sleeper is awakening! Like
the breeze from the Himalayas, it is bringing life into
the almost dead bones and muscles, the lethargy is
passing away, and only the blind cannot see, or the
perverted will not see, that she is awakening, this
motherland of ours, from her deep long sleep. None
can resist her anymore; never is she going to sleep any
more; no outward powers can hold her back any more;
for the infinite giant is rising to her feet."[97]

Sister Nivedita writes in her book on Vivekananda,
'The Master As I Saw Him":

"Throughout those years in which I saw him almost
daily, the thought of India was to him like the air he
breathed. He neither used the word nationality' nor
proclaim an era of nation making. 'Man Making' he
said was his own task. But he was born a lover, and the
queen of his adoration was his Motherland. Like some
delicately poised bell, thrilled and vibrated by every
sound that falls upon it, was his heart to all that
concerned her. Not a sob was heard within her shores
that did not find in him a responsive echo. There was
no cry or fear, no tremor of weakness, no shrinking
from mortification that he had not known and
understood. He was hard on her sins, unsparing of her
wants of worldly wisdom, but because he felt these faults
to be his own. And none on the contrary, was so ever
possessed by the vision of her greatness. To him she
appeared, as the giver of English civilization. For what,
he would ask , had been the England of Elizabeth in
comparison with the India of Akbar? Nay what would
England of Victoria have been without the wealth of
India, behind her."[98]

97. *Lectures From Colombo to Almora*, p-48.
98. Nivedita, *The Master As I Saw Him*, p-50.

Why is it…that forty millions of Englishmen rule three hundred millions of people here? What is the psychological explanation? These forty millions put their wills together and that means infinite power, and you three hundred millions have a will each separate from the other. Therefore to make a great future of India, the whole secret lies in organization, accumulation of power, coordination of wills…Being of one mind is the secret of society. And the more you go on fighting and quarrelling about tall trivialities such as 'Dravidian' and Aryan' and the question of Brahmanas and non-Brahmanas and all that the further you are off from that accumulation of energy and power which is going to make the future of India.

He saw before him a great Indian nationality, young, vigorous, fully the equal of any nationality on the face of the earth.[99]

When he was dubbed as a dreamer, he stated; "You are at liberty my friend to think that I am a dreamer, a visionary; but believe at least that I am sincere to the backbone, and my greatest fault is that I love my country only too, too well."[100]

During his stay in the west, he learnt that without organization and coordination of wills, success is not possible in any venture. He imparted this lesson to his countrymen:

"Why is it…that forty millions of Englishmen rule three hundred millions of people here? What is the psychological explanation? These forty millions put their wills together and that means infinite power, and you three hundred millions have a will each separate from the other. Therefore to make a great future of India, the whole secret lies in organization, accumulation of power, coordination of wills…Being of one mind is the secret of society. And the more you go on fighting and quarrelling about tall trivialities such as 'Dravidian' and Aryan' and the question of Brahmanas and non-Brahmanas and all that the further you are off from that accumulation of energy and power which is going to make the future of India."[101]

I read in the newspaper how, when one of our fellow is murdered or ill treated by an Englishman, howls go up all over the country; I read and I weep and the next moment comes to mind the question: who is responsible for it?[102]

We are responsible for what we are; and whatever we wish ourselves to be, we have the power to make ourselves. If what we are now has been the result of our past actions, it certainly follows that whatever we wish

99. Pravrajika, *Sister Nivedita*, p-71.
100. Letters, p-107.
101. C.W. Vol-III, 1948, p-299.
102. *Lectures From Colombo to Almora*, p-100.

to be in future can be produced by our present actions....[103]

It is the weakness that is the motive power in all evil doing; it is the weakness that is the source of all selfishness; it is weakness that makes men injure others; it is weakness that makes them manifest what they are not in reality. Let them all know what they are...Let them suck it in with their mother's milk, this idea of strength—I am He, and I am He.[104]

You can do anything. You fail only when you do not strive sufficiently to manifest infinite power. As soon as man or a nation loses faith in himself or itself, death comes. Believe first in yourself then in God.[105]

The man who says that he will work only when the world has become all good, and then he will enjoy bliss, is as likely to succeed as the man who sits besides a river and says, 'I shall cross when all the water has run into the ocean.'[106]

The wind is blowing; those vessels whose sails are unfurled, catch it and so they go forward on their way, but those whose sails are not unfurled, fail to catch the wind. Is that the fault of the wind? Blame neither man, or God, nor any one in the world, blame yourself and try to do better...All the strength and succor you need is within yourselves. Therefore, make your future.[107] Know that every thought and word that weakens you in this world is the only evil that exist. Whatever makes man weak and fear is the only evil that should be shunned. What can frighten you? If the sun come down and the moon crumble into dust...What is that to you? Stand as a rock; you are indestructible. You are the self, the God of the universe.[108]

> We are responsible for what we are; and whatever we wish ourselves to be, we have the power to make ourselves. If what we are now has been the result of our past actions, it certainly follows that whatever we wish to be in future can be produced by our present actions....

> The man who says that he will work only when the world has become all good, and then he will enjoy bliss, is as likely to succeed as the man who sits besides a river and says, "I shall cross when all the water has run into the ocean."

---

103. C.W. Vol-I, p-29, Vol-II, p-366.
104. C.W. Vol-III, p-426.
105. Letters, p-181.
106. C.W. Vol-II, p-140.
107. Ibid., p-324.
108. Ibid, p-236.

We shall crush the stars to atoms and unhinge the universe.[109]

Work with undaunted energy! What fear! Who is poweful enough to thwart you!"[110]

He stated that the only religion to be taught, is the religion of fearlessness. "Either in this world or in the world of religion, it is true that fear is the cause of degradation and sin. It is fear that brings misery, fear that brings death. And what causes fear? Ignorance of our own nature. Each one of us is heir-apparent to the Emperor of Emperors; we are of the substance of God Himself.[111]

Be not afraid of anything. You will do marvellous work. The moment you fear, you are nobody. It is fear that is the great cause of misery in the world. It is the fear that is the greatest of all superstitions. It is the fear, which is the cause of our woes, and it is the fearlessness that brings heaven even in a moment. Therefore, arise, awake and stop not till the goal is reached."[112]

He asked Indians to believe in themselves and to work out their goals without paying any heed to evil-teachings. Citing example of Lord Clive, the founder of English Empire in India, he said:

"In the history of each nation, you will always find that only those individuals who have believed in themselves have become great and strong. Here to India, came an Englishman who was only a clerk and for want of funds and other reasons he twice tried to blow his brain out; and when he failed, he believed in himself, he believed that he was born to do great things; and that man became Lord Clive, the founder of the Empire. If he had believed in the Padres and gone crawling all his life—'O Lord, I am weak and I am low'—where he would have been? In a lunatic asylum. You also are made lunatics by these evil teachings. I

---

109. Letters, p-135.
110. Ibid. p-182.
111. *Lectures From Colombo to Almora*, p-65.
112. C.W. Vol-III, p-321, 1948.

Sidenote: We shall crush the stars to atoms and unhinge the universe.

Sidenote: Be not afraid of anything. You will do marvellous work. The moment you fear, you are nobody. It is fear that is the great cause of misery in the world. It is the fear that is the greatest of all superstitions. It is the fear, which is the cause of our woes, and it is the fearlessness that brings heaven even in a moment. Therefore, arise, awake and stop not till the goal is reached.

have seen, all the world over, the bad effects of these weak teachings of humility destroying the human race. Our children are brought up in this way, and is it a wonder that they become semi-lunatics"?[113]

At Kumbhakonam, Vivekananda told his audience about his observations and understanding of the people of the West:

"...Inside the national hearts of both Europe and America, resides the tremendous power of men's faith in themselves. An English boy will tell you—I am an Englishman, and I can do anything and so will any boy. Can our boys say the same thing here? No nor even the boy's fathers—we have lost faith in ourselves.

If you have faith in all three hundred and thirty millions of your mythological gods...and still have no faith in yourselves, there is no salvation for you. Have faith in yourselves, and stand up on that faith and be strong; that is what we need."[114]

Along with the gospel of strength, he preached fearlessness and self-respect. This massage had a political significance. He said, "Let our physical bodies bear not a chicken heart, slavish desire, but mind made of thunderbolt, manhood.

> *"Go forward without a path;*
> *Even as the lion, not trembling at noises,*
> *Even as the wind, not caught in a net,*
> *Even as the lotus-leaf contained water,*
> *Do thou wander alone, like the rhinoceros.*[115]

"...This is not the time with us to weep even in joy; we have had weeping enough; no more is this the time to become soft. This softness has been with us till we have become like masses of cotton and are dead. What our country now wants are muscles of iron and nerves of steel, gigantic wills, which nothing can resist with.[116]

113. Ibid., p-427.
114. Ibid., p-190.
115. Life. Vol-I, 1979, p-264.
116. C.W. Vol-III, p-190.

Come up, O lions, and shake of the delusion that you are sheep; you are souls immortal, spirit free, blest and eternal. Ye are not matter, Ye are not bodies, matter is your servent, not you the servant of the matter.

The hour of action has sounded. Let us join our forces. We must shake of the lethargy that is stifling us— we who have become a mass of slaves, without power or freedom, without life and without will.[117]

Come up, O lions, and shake of the delusion that you are sheep; you are souls immortal, spirit free, blest and eternal. Ye are not matter, Ye are not bodies, matter is your servent, not you the servant of the matter."[118]

During the last years of his life, when due to his unfavourable health, he was not in a condition to tour the entire country, he pinned his hopes on the youth of Bengal:

"Arise awake and stop not till the desired end is reached. Young men of Calcutta, arise, awake, for the time is propitious. ..Be bold and fear not. We have to become Abhih, fearless and our task will be done. Arise, awake for your country needs this tremendous sacrifice. It is the young men that will do it...And we have hundreds and thousands of such young men in Calcutta. If I have done so much, how much more will you do!"[119]

He exhorted them to take over the leadership of the country.

"In other parts of India, there is intellect, there is money, but enthusiasm is only in my motherland. That must come out; therefore arise, young men of Calcutta, with enthusiasm in your blood. Think not that you are poor, that you have no friends. Ay, who ever saw money make the man? It is man that always makes money. The whole world has been made by the energy of man, by the power of enthusiasm, by the power of faith....I have done nothing as yet; you have to do the task. If I die tomorrow the work will not die. I sincerely believe that there will be thousands coming up from the ranks to take up the work and carry it further and further,

---

117. Reymond, p-104.
118. *Service and Spirituality*, p-94.
119. C.W. Vol-III, 1948, p-318

beyond all my hopeful imaginations ever painted. I have faith in my country, and especially in the youth of my country. The youth of Bengal have the greatest of all tasks that has ever been placed on the shoulders of young men.[120]

"Ye young Bengal, emulate the manly way of Laxmi Bai, the Rani of Jhansi, whose gallantry the English commander has recognized. Imitate the virtue of other nations, cultivate their technical skill and qualities of life...And then, with a modern standard of morale and efficiency attain, pay them, the foreign usurpers, in their own coins in your country to unfasten the alien octopus...[121]

Say I am Existence...I am He' and like a lion breaking its cage, break your chain and be free for ever."[122]

To impart consiousness among his countrymen, he started two bi-weekly journals in English named *Brahmavadin* and *Prabuddha Bharat* (Awakened India) and a Bengali magazine *Udbodhan*. He contributed a number of articles to all these journals:

Let us all work hard, my brethren.... On our work depends the coming of the India of future...Arise and Awake, and see her seated there, on her eternal throne, rejuvenated, more glorious than ever she was—this motherland of ours.[123]

Multitude counts for nothing. A few heart whole sincere and energetic man can do more in a year than a mob in a century. If there is a heat in one body, then those others that come near it must catch it. This is the law. So success is yours, so long as we keep the heat...[124]

...Are great things ever done smoothly? I could have told you many things that could have made your heart

> Let us all work hard, my brethren.... On our work depends the coming of the India of future...Arise and Awake, and see her seated there, on her eternal throne, rejuvenated, more glorious than ever she was—this motherland of ours.

> ...Are great things ever done smoothly? I could have told you many things that could have made your heart leap, but I will not. I want iron wills and hearts that do not know how to quake.

120. Ibid, p-318-320.
121. Datta, p-333.
122. C.W. Vol-II, p-236.
123. C.W. Vol-III, p-154.
124. Letters, p-233.

leap, but I will not. I want iron wills and hearts that do not know how to quake."[125]

Knowing this, stand up and fight! Not one step back, that is idea...Fight it out, whatever comes. Let the stars move from the sphere! Let the whole world stand against us! Thus fight! You gain nothing by becoming cowards...Taking a step backward, you do not avoid any misfortune. You have cried to all the gods in the world. Has misery ceased? The masses in India cry to six million gods, and still die like dogs. Where are these gods?...The god comes to help you when you have succeeded. So what is the use. Die game... This bending the knee to superstitions, this selling yourself to your own mind does not befit you...You are infinite spirit it does not befit you to be slave....Arise, Awake! Stand up and fight.![126] "Defeat is better than a vegetating ignorant life; it is better to die in a battle field than to live a life of defeat.[127]

Be not in despair, the way is very difficult like walking on the edge of a razor; yet despair not; arise, awake and find the goal.[128]

Up, up. The long night is passing, the day is approaching; the wave has risen, nothing will be able to resist its tidal fury. Believe, believe, the decree has gone forth, the fiat of the Lord has gone forth—India must rise, the masses and the poor are to be made happy. Rejoice![129]

Revealing his plans he said: "I have come to you my children, to tell you all my plans. If you hear them I am ready to work with you. But if you will not listen to them, and even kick me out of India, I will come back and tell you that we are all sinking."[130]

125. Ibid., p-242.
126. C.W. Vol-I, p-461.
127. C.W. Vol-II, p-124, 1968.
128. C.W. Vol-III, p-27, 1948.
129. C.W. Vol-V, p-29.
130. *Lectures From Colombo to Almora*, p-140.

Thou too clad with but a rag sound thy lions proudly proclaim at the top of the voice, 'The Indian is my brother, the Indian is my life, India's gods and goddesses are my God, India's society is the cradle of my infancy, the pleasure garden of my youth, the sacred heaven; Varanasi of my old age; say brother, the soil of India is my highest heaven, the good of India is my good and repeat and pray day and night, 'O thou Lord of Gauri, O Thou Mother of the Universe, vouchsafe manliness unto me! O thou Mother of Strength, take away my weakness, take away my unmanliness and Make me a Man!"[131]

He preached that India belongs to all its inhabitants and all are the children of Mother India. Knowing the power and hold of the religion on the people, he asked his disciples to impart political awareness through religion:

"If you want to speak of politics in India, you must speak through the language of religion. You have to tell them (people) something like this—he will go to heaven.

The man who cleans his house every morning will acquire such and such an amount of merit, he will go to heaven, or he comes to God. Unless you put it that way, they won't listen to you."[132]

He used to recite verses from Vedas, Upanishads, Koran and Bible. His audience included Hindus, Sikhs as well as Muslims.[133]

Later Gandhi followed Vivekananda and used to recite verses from various religious scriptures in his prayer meetings.

Though, the majority in Vivekananda's meetings used to be hindus and he preached patriotism through Hinduism yet he cannot be the Guru of the advocates of the Hindu Rashtra because in his view, it is not only religion but the community of feeling and of

> If you want to speak of politics in India, you must speak through the language of religion. You have to tell them (people) something like this—he will go to heaven.

> The man who cleans his house every morning will acquire such and such an amount of merit, he will go to heaven, or he comes to God. Unless you put it that way, they won't listen to you.

---

131. C.W. Vol-IV, p-412, 413.
132. *Centenary Celebrations*, p-1962-63, p-272.
133. *Life*-Vol-I, p-121.

Man can never be united unless there is a bond of common interest, you can never unite people merely by getting up meetings, societies and lectures, if their interest be not one and the same...Guru Gobind Singh made it understood everywhere that the men of his age, be they Hindus or Mussalmans were living under a regime of profound injustice and oppression. He did not create any common interest, he only pointed it out to the masses. And so both Hindus and Muslims followed him.

aspirations, that makes a nation. 'Besides for nation making' he said, 'fusion of different races and tribes and acceptance of different customs, religions and languages, is essential as out of such fusion is born the true national spirit which can be enduring'[134]

He was also against the imposition of a common language upon the linguistic minorities.[135]

He appealed to all Indians to unite for the national cause and shed narrow divisions based on caste, region and religion:

"Man can never be united unless there is a bond of common interest, you can never unite people merely by getting up meetings, societies and lectures, if their interest be not one and the same...Guru Gobind Singh made it understood everywhere that the men of his age, be they Hindus or Mussalmans were living under a regime of profound injustice and oppression. He did not create any common interest, he only pointed it out to the masses. And so both Hindus and Muslims followed him."[136]

Giving a call for national solidarity, he said:

"Thou brave one, be bold, take courage, be proud that thou art an Indian and proudly proclaim; I am an Indian, every Indian is my brother.

Root out of your narrow holes and have a look broad. See how nations are on the march. Do you love man? Do you love your country? Then come, let us struggle for higher and better things, look not back, no not even if you see the dearest cry. Look not back but forward.[137]

Even in politics and sociology problems that were national twenty years ago can no longer be solved on national grounds only. These are assuming whole proportions and gigantic shape. They can only be

134. C.W. Vol-IV, p-308, 316.
135. C.W. Vol-IV, p-309.
136. *Talks with Swami Vivekananda*, p-86.
137. C.W. Vol-V, p-8, 1947.

solved when looked at in the broader light of international grounds. International organizations, international combinations, international laws are the cry of the day. There cannot be any progress without the whole world 'being based on truth and justice. It is becoming everyday clearer that the solution of any problem can never be attained on racial, national or narrow grounds. Every idea has become broad till it covers the whole of the world, every aspiration must go on increasing, till it has engulfed the whole humanity— I am thoroughly convinced that no individual or nation can live by holding itself apart from the community of others. Colonialism breeds exclusiveness. This is the main cause of the degradation of man today. All nations must get back into the world current."[138]

He thus advocated progressive, secular and international approach for solving any problem. Looking back was not the solution, it would only cause national decay and death:

"We have either to go forward or to backward. We have either to progress or to degenerate. Our ancestors did great things in the past, but we have to grow into fuller life and march beyond even their great achievements. How can we now go back and degenerate ourselves? That cannot be; that must not be; going back will lead to national decay and death.[139]

The dead cannot be reborn. The night that has ended cannot be brought back. Enthusiasm once lost can be revived but never to the same pitch. O Man! I invite you to turn from a veneration of what is sterile and dead to what is full of life and promise. I invite you to turn from regretting over past mistakes to consolidating our present task. I urge you not to waste any more effort over retrieving obscure remedies but to join whole heartedly in the newly founded national effort. For the intelligent, no more need be said.[140]

> We have either to go forward or to backward. We have either to progress or to degenerate. Our ancestors did great things in the past, but we have to grow into fuller life and march beyond even their great achievements. How can we now go back and degenerate ourselves? That cannot be; that must not be; going back will lead to national decay and death.

---

138. *Lectures From Colombo to Almora*, p-155-56.
139. C.W. Vol-III, p-195, 196.
140. C.W. Vol-VI, p-188, 1956.

Vivekananda celebrated 4th of July, the American Independence Day with his disciples by writing and reciting a poem, the central theme of the poem was the yearning for freedom. The concluding stanza:

> 'Move on, oh Lord, in the resistless path
> Till the high noon o'er spreads the world;
> Till every land reflects thy light;
> Till men and women with uplifted head
> Behold their shackles broken, and Know, in
> their springing joy their life renewed".[141]

He went to Paris in October, 1900. He was accompanied by Sister Nivedita. There he met several public figures including Sir Hiram Maxim, inventor of the machine-gun, from whom in his youth he had learnt the art of gun making. What did they converse is not known. However, it seems that his faith in the efficacy of revolutionary means became firmer. The Swami, on his return from west the second time told a youngman at Belur, that "what India needs today is a bomb."[142]

He admired Chapekar brothers of Pune who had murdered Mr. Rand and Mr. Ayerst of the Plague Commission who had dishonoured Indian women in the name of medical examination. Chapekar brothers admitted that they had intentionally murdered Rand. They also stated in the court that they had earlier disfigured the marble statue of Queen Victoria in Bombay. Chapekar brothers were convicted and sentenced to death. Vivekanand enquired of Tilak when the latter visited him at his *Math* that why a memorial was not being made for the martyrs who had been hanged for their patriotism. He suggested that golden statues of these martyrs be erected at the India Gate in Bombay.[143] Later, Sister Nivedita went

---

141. Bhupendra Nath Roy, *Nivedita*, Pub-Mahto West Bengal, year, N.M. p-5.
142. Datta, p-212.
143. *Nivedita Commemoration* Vol. ed. by Amiya Kr. Majumdar, Pub-Vivekananda Janamasthan Samiti, 1968 Calcutta, p-88.

to Poona and met Chapekar brother's mother and saluted her.

Vivekananda and Tilak were also in touch with Mataji Maharani Tapswini, a contemporary of Laxmi Bai of Jhansi, who was also her aunt. Both had fought on horse-back in the revolt of 1857. It is reported that after the failure of revolt she escaped to Nepal with Nana Saheb. She continued her activities from there and kept in touch with the revolutionaries including Vivekananda. She came back to Calcutta secretly in 1901 and set up a factory to manufacture arms. She met Tilak who was in the city in connection with the Congress session. Though there is no evidence of any meeting between Vivekananda and the Maharani but it confirms that Vivekananda was a revolutionary patriot and in close touch with other revolutionaries both in India and abroad.[144]

In 1902, a Japanese revolutionary named Kakuzo came to Calcutta, to invite Vivekananda to Japan. He also met and addressed some Bengali students and in a well-attended meeting stated: "You are such a great and cultured race. Why do you let a handful of Englishmen tread you down? Do everything you can to achieve freedom openly as well as secretly. Japan will assist you."[145] It is significant that he stayed in the monastery as the swami's guest. Vivekananda also accompanied Kakuzo to Bodh Gaya.

Sister Nivedita writes:

"In India he was more a patriot, a worker for the regeneration of his motherland with all the struggle and torture of a lion caught in a net...Forced to live a comparatively retired life in the monastery, he put his noble soul to the task of making workers carry out his plans and ideas."[146]

In India he was more a patriot, a worker for the regeneration of his motherland with all the struggle and torture of a lion caught in a net...Forced to live a comparatively retired life in the monastery, he put his noble soul to the task of making workers carry out his plans and ideas.

---

144. Satyavarta, Ghose, *Remembering our Revolutionaries* Marxist Study Forum, Hyderabad, 199, p-66.
145. Peter Heens, *Nationalism, Terrorism, Communism* Oxford Uni. Calcutta, 1998, p-72.
146. Moni Bagchee, *Sister Nivedita*, Pub-Anil Chanda Calcutta 1958, p-37.

Yes! The older I grow, the more everything seems to me to lie in manliness. This is my new gospel. Do even evil like a man! Be wicked, if you must, on a grand scale!

His yearning for freedom increased with each passing day and so his belief in manliness. Sister, Nivedita mentions him saying once during his last days: "Yes! The older I grow, the more everything seems to me to lie in manliness. This is my new gospel. Do even evil like a man! Be wicked, if you must, on a grand scale!"[147]

Face nature! Face ignorance! Face illusion! Never fly! You remember the story of the king who saw the vision of an enchanted palace, and when he spat on the ground it vanished!

Numerous students from schools and colleges used to visit *Math* to seek his guidance and the latter used to say, "Face nature! Face ignorance! Face illusion! Never fly! You remember the story of the king who saw the vision of an enchanted palace, and when he spat on the ground it vanished!"[148]

To inculcate spirit of heroism, Vivekananda used to quote from Madhusudan Dutt's *Meghnadbadh Kavya*, which glorified the heroic spirit of Ravana. He had this book in the *Math* Library.

"Indrajit was slain in the battle and Mandodari, the wife of the King Ravana, stricken with sorrow at the loss of her valiant son, is imploring her husband to desist from battle; but Ravana, like a great hero that he is, casting off from his heart all grief for his dead son, and without caring for the fate of his queen and other sons, is ready to go out for battle, burning with pride, anger and revenge! 'Let whatever come as it may, let the universe remain or be broken up into fragments, I will not forget my duty!- these are the words of a mighty hero!"[149]

No rest! I shall die in harness...Let me live and die fighting.[150] and I shall consider it a great honour, if I had to go through hell in doing good to my country.

Despite his ill-health, his spirit remained undiminished. His asthma had worsened, his kidneys were affected by diabetes—he was aware of that. He was advised rest by the doctors but his spirit could not rest. "No rest! I shall die in harness...Let me live and die fighting."[150] and "I shall consider it a great honour, if I had to go through hell in doing good to my country".[151]

147. C.W. Vol-VIII, 1959, p-264.
148. Life. Vol-III, p-64.
149. *Last Days of Swami Vivekananda*, p-59.
150. Choudhry, p-105.
151. Ibid.,

He expressed this hope again in his address to the students of M.E. School, Belur, where he had been invited to distribute prizes. Speaking on 22nd January, 1901, Vivekananda remarked that the future of India depends upon them . 'I do not despair, I am seeing a glorious and wonderful future in my menial visions."[152]

He had observed the volcanic situation which could, if ignited, blast the British rule. He foresaw the possibility of revolution in near future. Despite ill-health, he visited Dacca in 1901 and there in a public meeting he advised the youth:

"Be strong my young friends; that is my advice to you. You will be nearer to Heaven through football, then through the study of Gita. You will understand Gita better with your bicep muscles a little stronger. The Gita was taught not to an unmanly lot of man, but to Arjuna, a great warrior, the leader of the warlike race of Kshtriyas. You will understand the mighty genius and the mighty strength of Krishna with a little of strong blood in you. You will understand the Upanishads better and the glory of Atman, when your body stands firm upon your feet and you feel yourselves as men."[153]

At Dacca some students including Hemchandra Ghose, who later became a well-known revolutionary, Sirspal, Maulvi Alimuddin, Jogendra Nath Datta went to him to seek guidance. Vivekanand told them that India was no more a Punyabhumi but the land of Jo-Hukums (subserviency to the master's will), the land of serfs and slaves.: "Your duty should be service to motherland, India should be freed politically first."[154]

He also said: "Man-making is my mission of life Hemchandra! You try with your comrades to translate this mission of mine into reality" and "a slave nation had no religion except to acquire strength and drive out the usurper of power". He told pandit Sakahram Ganesh Deuskar, a revolutionary, "The country has become a Powder Magazine. A little spark may ignite it, I will see the revolution in life time."[155]

Man-making is my mission of life Hemchandra! You try with your comrades to translate this mission of mine into reality.

152. *Vivekananda in Indian Newspapers*, p-215.
153. C.W. Vol-III, p-243, 1948, *Vivekananda in Indian Newspapers*, p-577.
154. Datta, p-333-34.
155. Ibid., p-IX.

His fiery words produced patriotic heat and whoso-
ever came near, could not escape its revolutionary
impact. He would burst like hurricane on his audience.
Numerous students gave up their studies and followed
the path carved out by their hero. They decided to
dedicate their lives at the altar of Mother India.
Hemchandra, Ganesh Deuskar, Bagha Jatin (Mukherjee),
Jyotindra Nath, and many others stepped up their
revolutionary activities and gave the authorities many
sleepless nights. Vivekananda died in July 1902. Within
three years of his death concrete efforts were made to
wrest freedom by revolutionary means. The revolutionary fervour engulfed entire Bengal, Bombay and
Punjab. Numerous secret revolutionary societies were
formed. Arms were procured and bombs manufactured.
The slogan 'Vande Matram' (worship motherland)
rented the sky. The spirit of fearlessness preached by
Vivekananda manifested everywhere. Sister Nivedita
whom he counted to arouse political awareness among
Indians and it was in this sense that he pledged her to
serve India, left the spiritual fold and joined the revolutionary upsurge, a fortnight after Vivekananda's
death.[156] Many Swamis of the *Math*, he had established,
too were found visiting the secret societies and addressing the youth. "It might be that the main theme of their
teachings...was the building of character; but it would
be idle to presume that these swamis were totally
unaware of the real objectives of the samities."[157] The
Ramakrishna Mission and its branches in Eastern
Bengal, according to the British secret reports, served
double purpose of providing a meeting place to revolutionary leaders and centre for recruiting new members
for the revolutionary work.[158] Patriotic speeches and
writings of Vivekananda became 'Bible' for all the
revolutionaries and were found in every house of the
revolutionaries during the upsurge of 1905. It was the
first attempt made by the revolutionaries to translate
the mission of Vivekananda into reality.

155. Ibid., p-IX.
156. Reymond, p-262.
157. Arun Chandra Guha, *First Spark of the Revolution* Orient Longman, N.D. 1971, p-80.
158. S.C. Sen Gupta, *Swami Vivekananda and Indian Nationalism*, p-107.

Masiha of the Masses

"I do not believe in a God or religion which cannot wipe the widow's tears or bring a piece of bread to the orphan's mouth."

— **Swami Vivekananda**

Vivekananda was a well-read man and knew very well that the end of the foreign rule would not end the exploitation and the misery of the common masses. Hence, he advocated socialism for independent India as it was the only system, though not perfect, for ensuring justice to all the downtrodden of the country.

Vivekananda introduced the word socialism in India. He proclaimed himself to be a socialist. He said: "I am a socialist not because I think it is a perfect system, but half a loaf is better than no bread."[1]

Though there is no evidence that he had read 'Das Capital' or 'The Communist Manifesto' of Marx yet his writings and speeches make it evident that he was well acquainted with the literature of the socialist revolutionaries of Europe and had met some of them. Sister Nivedita, who accompanied him during his second visit to West, introduced him to some of the prominent revolutionaries and philosophers including Kropotkin, the propounder of Anarchism. Kropotkin was a famous Russian revolutionary living in exile. Vivekananda met him in Paris in August 1900 and discussed India's condition with him. In London, he met Edward Carpenter and other Socialist Democrats. He also knew Bakunin, another prominent socialist

---

1. C.W. Vol-VI, 1956, p-381.

156   *Swami Vivekananda–An Iconoclastic Ascetic*

leader of Russia.[2] Like a socialist, he exhorted the masses to arise, awake and assert for their rights and foretold that the Proletocult (Proletarian culture) of the masses would be the future of New India.

However, it was not the knowledge of the concept but the sufferings of the people, which made Vivekananda, an advocate of Socialism. Five years of wandering all over the country on foot made him familiar with the real face of India. He was deeply moved by the miserable state of the ignorant masses who had taken it as their fate. Besides, he himself had experienced acute financial hardships after his father's death. Despitebing qualified, he did not get a job. This personal encounter with the ugly face of the then economic system made him an opponent of capitalism. In Madras, near the sea-side he saw "the wretched and half starved children of fishermen, working with their mother, waist-deep in water. Vivekananda's kind heart and rational outlook could not bear this, tears filled in his eyes and he cried out 'O Lord why dost Thou create these miserable creatures! I cannot bear the sight of them."[3]

He had searched God in temples, caves, and mountains but did not find Him there. However at Kanyakumari, he found his God. His god was not almighty but helpless,oppressed and suppressed since ages. He was poor and needed services of Vivekananda and the later decided to dedicate his life for his newly discovered God.

He coined the word 'Daridranarayana' later used by Gandhiji. He said to himself, "We are so many sanyasins wandering about and teaching the people metaphysics—it is all madness...That those people who are leading the life of brutes is simply due to ignorance."[4] Like his master, Swami Ramakrishna,

2. *Nivedita Commemoration*, ed. by Amiya Kumar Majumdar, Pub-Vivekananda Janamsthan, 1968, Calcutta, p-53.
3. *Life*, Vol-I, 1979, p-365.
4. C.W. Vol-VI, 1956, p-254.

Vivekananda too realised that no religion would satisfy the cravings of hunger. Thence upon he gave up all the wish for his own salvation and declared:

"I have lost all wish for my salvation. May I born again and again and suffered thousand of miseries so that I may worship the only God that exists, the only God that I believe in, the sum total of all souls...my God the poor of all races... Him worship, the visible, the knowable, omnipresent; break all other idols."[5]

He exclaimed 'Ye ever trampled labouring masses of India! I bow to you"[6]

Castigating the religious authorities and the religion for the pitiable condition of the Indian masses, he said:

"A country where millions of people live on the flower of the Mahua plant and a million or two sadhus and hundred millions or so of Brahmins suck the blood out of these poor people...is that a country or hell? Is that a religion or the devil dance."[7]

Speaking about his own belief, he declared:

"I do not believe in a God or religion which cannot wipe the widow's tears or bring a piece of bread to the orphan's mouth. However sublime be the theories, however well spun may be the philosophy—I do not call it a religion...[8] I call a mahatma (great soul) whose heart bleeds for the poor, otherwise he is duratman. (Wicked soul)[9]"

Indignantly rejecting the argument that by giving up comforts here and now one can ensure eternal happiness in the life to come—an argument that has been used for centuries to justify social injustice and oppression—Vivekananda snapped, "I do not believe in a God who will give me undying bliss in Heaven, but who cannot give me bread in this world."[10]

5. C.W. Vol-V, 1947, p-166.
6. Ibid. Vol-III, 1948, p-241.
7. C.W. Vol-VI, 1956, p-254.
8. C.W. Vol-V, 1947.
9. Ibid., p-58.
10. C.W. Vol-V, 1947, p-45.

Lamenting over the helplessness of the poor-people, he said, "Oh my heart ached to think of what we think of the poor, the low in India. They have no chance, no escape, no way to climb up. The poor, the low, the sinner in India have no friends, no help, they cannot rise...They sink lower and lower, everyday, they feel the blows showering upon them by a cruel society...They have forgotton that they are too men."[11]

Raising the masses became his religion and he looked for ways to rescue them from all kinds of exploitation.

Like a Marxist, he divided the society into two classes i.e. the upper and the lower class. The latter class, he designated as the masses or the Shudras. He condemned the upper classes of India for exploiting the poor, he said:

"Our aristocratic ancestors went on treading masses of our country under foot, till they became helpless, till under their torment the poor people nearly forgot that they were human beings. They have been compelled to be merely hewers of wood and drawers of water for centuries, so much so that they are made to believe that they are born as slaves, born as hewers of wood and drawers of water."[12]

He admonished the aristocracy for their false pride in birth and ancestory and condemned its existence in the following words:

"However, much you may parade your descent from Aryan ancestors and sing the glories of ancient India day and night, and however much you may be strutting in the pride of your birth, you the upper classes of India, do you think you are alive? You are but mummies the thousand years old...and it is you who are the real walking corpses...You represent the past tense, with all its varieties of form jumbled into one. That one still seems to see you at the present time, is nothing but a nightmare brought on by indigestion. You are the void,

> Our aristocratic ancestors went on treading masses of our country under foot, till they became helpless, till under their torment the poor people nearly forgot that they were human beings. They have been compelled to be merely hewers of wood and drawers of water for centuries, so much so that they are made to believe that they are born as slaves, born as hewers of wood and drawers of water.

11. Letters, p-67.
12. *Lectures From Colombo to Almora*, p-101.

the unsubstantiated nonentities of the future. Denizens of the dreamland, why are you loitering any longer? Fleshless and bloodless skeletons of the dead body of past India that you are, why do you not quickly reduce yourself into dust and disappear in the air."[13]

The upper classes had not only socially and economically enslaved the masses since ages but were also responsible for India's enslavement. He said:

"It is simply due to your having despised the masses of India that you have now been living a life of slavery for the last thousand years; it is therefore that you are objects of hatred in the eyes of foreigners and are looked upon with indifference by your countrymen."[14]

Like Karl Marx, he too felt that the aristocratic class digs its own grave; and the sooner it does so, the better. The more it delays, the more it shall fester and the worse death it will die. Warning the upper classes he said:

"You will be destroyed by the internecine quarrels and fights which you have been having so long. When the masses will wake up, they will come to understand your oppression of them and by a puff of their mouth you will be entirely blown away! It is they who have introduced civilization amongst you and it is they who will then pull it down. Think how at the hands of the Gauls the mighty ancient Roman civilization crumbled into dust![15]

The peasant, the shoe maker, the sweeper, and such other lower classes of India have much greater capacity for work and self-reliance than you. They have been silently working through ages and producing the entire wealth of the land, without a word of complaint. You have so long oppressed these forbearing masses; now is the time for retribution.[16]

---

13. Ibid.,
14. C.W. Vol-VII, p-170-72.
15. Ibid., p-150.
16. Benoy Kumar Roy, *Socio-Political Views of Swami Vivekananda* APPH. N.D. 1970, p-32-33.

Let New India arise in your place. Let her arise—out of the peasant's cottage, grasping the plough; out of the huts of the fishermen, the cobbler and the sweeper. Let her sprung from the grocer's shop, from beside the oven of the fritter-seller. Let her emanate from the factory, from marts and from markets. Let her emerge from groves and forests, from hills and mountains. These common people have suffered oppression for thousand of years—suffered it without murmur....They have suffered eternal misery, which has given them unflinching vitality, living on a handful of grain, they can convulse the world....Throw these treasure-chest of yours and those jewelled rings among them as soon as you can; and you vanish into the air, and be seen no more—only keep your ears open. No sooner will you disappear than you will hear the inaugural shout of renaissant India."[17]

Pointing out the deplorable condition of the labourers who had been working for the comforts of the upper classes for ages, he said:

"And where are they through whose physical labour only are possible, the influence of the Brahman, the prowess of the Kshatriya and the fortune of the Vaishya? What is their history, who being the real body of the society, are designated, at all times, in all countries, as 'base-born? For whom kind India prescribed the mild punishments, 'Cut out his tongue, chop off his flesh' for such a grave offence as any attempt on their part to gain a share of the knowledge and wisdom monopolised by her higher classes...[18]

If these lower classes stop work, from where will you get food and clothing? If the sweepers of Calcutta stop work for a day, it creates panic; and if they strike for three days, the whole town will be depopulated by the outbreak of epidemics. If the labourers stop work, your supply of food and clothes also stops. And you regard them as low-class people and vaunt your own culture."[19]

17. C.W. Vol-VII, 1947, p-309-10.
18. C.W. Vol-IV, 1946, p-400.
19. C.W. Vol-VII, 1947, p-148.

He regarded the labouring classes as the backbone of the country, who by their blood had contributed to the progress of the country had given rise to a brisk international trade between India and the outside world. Adressing the labouring classes of India, he exclaimed:

"Ye, labouring classes of India, as a result of your silent, constant labour Babylon, Persia, Alexandria, Greece, Rome, Venice, Genoa, Baghdad, Samarkand, Spain, Protugal, France, Denmark, Holland and England have successively attained supremacy and eminence. And you?—well who cares to think for you. My dear swami, your ancestors wrote a few philosophical works, penned a dozens or so epics, or built a number of temples—that is all, and you rend the skies with triumphal shouts; while those whose heart's blood has contributed to all the progress that has been made in this world-well, who cares to praise them.?"[20]

However, Vivekananda interpreted the Indian history in terms of caste rule and not on the basis of class. First was the rule by Brahmins and the second by Kshatriyas and the then existing was that of Vaishyas. Whether the rulers were Brahmins, Kshatriyas or the Vaishyas, exploitation and oppression of the masses remained same. Writing about the *Vaishya's* power, which in India was represented by the then British rulers, he stated:

"That mighty newly arise Vaishya power—at whose command, electricity carries messages in an instant from one pole to another, whose highway is the vast ocean, with its mountain-high waves, at whose instance comodities are being carried with the greatest ease from one part of the globe to another, and at whose mandate, even the greatest monarchs tremble on the white foamy crest of that huge wave, the all conquering Vaishya power, is installed the majestic throne of England in all its grandeur.[21]

---

20. Ibid., p-340.
21. C.W. Vol-IV, 1948, p-451-52.

"For self-preservation, the Vaishya, as a body, are, therefore, of one mind. The Vaishya commands the money; the exorbitant interest that he can extract for its use by others, as with a lash in his hand, is his powerful weapon which strikes terror in the heart of all. By the power of his money, he is always busy curbing the royal power. That the royal power may not anyhow stand in the way of the inflow of his riches, the merchant is ever watchful. But, for all that he has never the least wish that the power should pass from the kingly to the shudra (proletarian) class."[22]

According to him the conquest of India by England lay in economic reasons:

"Behind the name of the Lord Jesus, the Bible, the magnificient palaces, the heavy tramp of the feet of the armies consisting elephants, chariots, cavalry and infantry, shaking the earth, the sounds of war trumpets, bugles and drums and the splendid display of the royal throne, behind all these, there is the virtual presence of England...whose Empress is the shining Goddess of Fortune herself."[23]

Travelling through the cities of America and Europe, Vivekananda saw the people living in comforts and enjoying their lives. He shed tears on the poor state of his countrymen. He cried:

"O Mother, what do I care for name or fame, when my motherland remains sunk in utmost poverty! To what a sad pass have we poor Indians come, when millions of us die for want of a handful of rice, and here they spent millions of rupees upon their personal comfort! Who will raise the masses of India? Who will give them bread? Show me, O Mother, how can I help them."[24]

The contrast between the condition of the Indian masses and that of the west made him ponder and he

Margin note: Behind the name of the Lord Jesus, the Bible, the magnificient palaces, the heavy tramp of the feet of the armies consisting elephants, chariots, cavalry and infantry, shaking the earth, the sounds of war trumpets, bugles and drums and the splendid display of the royal throne, behind all these, there is the virtual presence of England...whose Empress is the shining Goddess of Fortune herself.

22. C.W. Vol-IV, 1946, p-400.
23. Ibid., p-451-52.
24. D. S. Sarma, The Renaissance of Hinduism, p-273 Pub-Benaras Hindu University, 1944.

reached the conclusion that in the present state of the world unless his countrymen also gave a strong physical basis to their civilization, it will tumble down. He appreciated material civilization as it provided equal opportunity to all and bread to the poor.

"We talk foolishly against material civilization. The grapes are sour. Even taking all that foolishness for granted, in all India there are, say, a hundred thousand really spiritual men and women. Now, for the spiritualization of these, must three hundred millions be sunk in savagery and starvation? How was it possible for the Hindus to have been conquered by the Mohammedans? It was due to the Hindu ignorance of material civilization. Even the Mohammedans taught them to wear tailor made clothes.[25] Material civilization, nay, even luxury, is necessary to create work for the poor. Bread! Bread! I do not believe in a God who cannot give me bread here, giving eternal bliss in heaven! Pooh! India is to be raised, the poor are to be fed, education is to be spread, and the evil of priestcraft is to be removed. No social tyranny! More bread, more opportunity for everybody.[26]

First bread and then religion. What we want is not so much spirituality as a little of the bringing down of the Advaita into the material world. We stuff them too much with religion when the poor fellows have been starving. No dogma will satisfy the craving hunger."[27]

During his stay in western countries, he closely observed how capitalism had moved to imperialism. The leaders were engaged in shamelessly plundering the resources of the world, of the people of weak and backward colonial countries; which became especially ruthless at the close of the nineteenth century. He observed;

"There never was a time in the world's history when there was so much robbery and high handedness, and

---

25. C.W. Vol-IV, p-368.
26. Ibid.,
27. C.W. Vol-III, 1948, p-432.

tyranny of the strong over the weak, as at this latter end of the nineteenth century."[28]

The redistribution of colonies and sphere of influence was leading to a war-like situation among the rival imperialist groups, the ultimate sufferer would be the common masses. In his 'Memoirs of the European Travel' he wrote:

"In an evil hour, did France suffer defeat from Germany. Through anger and fear she made every citizen a soldier...In other countries also conscription has been introduced in mutual dread of one another—so throughout Europe, excepting only England. England being an island, is continually strenthening her navy...Russia has the largest population of all, so she can amass the biggest army in Europe...But who is to supply the funds? Consequently the peasants have had to put on tattered rags—while in the towns you will find soldiers dressed in gorgeous uniforms. Throughout Europe there is craze for soldiers—soldiers everywhere...[29]

They that have money kept the government of land under their thumb, are robbing the people and sending them as soldiers to fight and to slain on foreign shores, so that in case of victory, their coffers may be full of gold bought by the blood of the subject people on the field of battle. And the subject-people? Well, theirs is only to shed their blood. That is politics."[30]

Vivekananda did not consider liberal democracy as prevalent in the western world suitable for independent India. During his stay in the west his sharp intellect dectected that the democracy existing there was a farce. It was not for the people or by the people. Exposing the real face of the western democratic system Vivekananda explained:

"The wealth and power of the country are in the hands of few who do not work but manipulate the work

> The wealth and power of the country are in the hands of few who do not work but manipulate the work of the millions of human beings; by this power, they deluge the whole earth with blood. Religion and all other things are under their feet; they rule and stand supreme. The western world is governed by a handful of Shylocks. All these things that you hear about-constitutional government, freedom, liberty and parliaments—are but jokes.

28. Benoy Kumar, p-46.
29. C.W. Vol-VII, p-374, 1947.
30. C.W. Vol-VI, 1956, p-462.

of the millions of human beings; by this power, they deluge the whole earth with blood. Religion and all other things are under their feet; they rule and stand supreme. The western world is governed by a handful of Shylocks. All these things that you hear about-constitutional government, freedom, liberty and parliaments—are but jokes."[31]

Speaking about the politicians, he said:

"If you ever saw that shocking sight behind the scene of acting of politicians—that revelry of bribery, that robbery in the broad daylight, that dance of the devil in man, which are practise on such occasions—you would be hopless about man."[32]

Along with the ugly face of the bourgeois democracy, he also discerned a new consciousness rising from the bottom of the society. The working class led by the best representatives of intellectuals was rising for a total transformation of the world and human society. Vivekananda made the Indians aware about this development. In his Colombo address he informed:

"That there are tremendous political movements and socialistic movements trying to transform western society, how many of you know? Very few indeed."[33]

Vivekananda expressed his hope that future will belong to the toiling masses. He foretold: "Yet a time will come when there will be the rising of the Sudra class...a time will come when the Sudra class...will gain absolute supremacy in every society.[34]

The first glow of the dawn of this new power has already begun to break slowly, upon the western world, and the thoughtful are at their wits end to reflect upon the final issue of this fresh phenomenon. Socialism, Anarchism, Nihilism, end other like sects are the vanguard of the social revolution that is to follow."[35]

31. C.W. Vol-I, 1970, p-158.
32. Ibid.,
33. C.W. Vol-III, 1948, p-277.
34. Datta, Bhupendranath, *Swami Vivekananda, Patriot-Prophet*, P-Introduction.
35. C.W. Vol-IV, 1948, p-468-69.

However in India there was no such upheavel. The masses were not only exploited and oppressed by the Britishers but also by the Indian feudal lords, the capitalists as well as by the religious leaders. They were illiterate, ignorant, had lost faith in themselves and looked upon God for everything. In that scenario it was not easy to arouse the masses, to make them aware about the reality and to fill in them ' the confidence', a pre-condition to build any movement. Besides, Vivekananda was a monk and knew about the constraints of monkhood. He could not openly work among the masses as it was bound to be taken as political work. He was also aware of the ever watchful eyes of the intelligence forces. Hence he chose monks and youth to carry out the work of raising the downtrodden. Using religious terminology, the masses were to be awakened. In his letters and lectures, he emphasized the need to work among the masses. In one such letter he wrote:

Let us throw away all this paraphernalia of worship—blowing the conch and ringing the bell, and waving the lights before the Images...Let us throw all the pride of learning and study of the shastras and all sadhanas for the attainment of personal mukti—and going from village to village devote our lives for the service of the poor.

"Where should you go to seek your God—are not all the poor, the miserable, the weak, Gods? Why not worship them first? Why go to dig a well on the shores of Ganga?[36]

The poor, the illiterate, the ignorant, the afflicted—let these be your God."[37]

He advised his disciples:

"Let us throw away all this paraphernalia of worship—blowing the conch and ringing the bell, and waving the lights before the Images...Let us throw all the pride of learning and study of the shastras and all sadhanas for the attainment of personal mukti—and going from village to village devote our lives for the service of the poor.[38]

Let the Vedas, the Koran, the Puranas and all scriptural lumber rest for some time, let there be

Let the Vedas, the Koran, the Puranas and all scriptural lumber rest for some time, let there be worship of the visible God of love and kindness in the country.

36. Ibid., p-368.
37. *Life* Vol-I, p-539, 1979.
38. Romain Rolland, The Life of *Swami Vivekananda and the Universal Gospel*, Advaita Ashram, Calcutta, 1931, p-164.

worship of the visible God of love and kindness in the country.

In yet another letter he wrote:

"After so much Tapasya I have known that the highest truth is this He is present in every thing! These are all the manifold forms of Him. There is no other God to seek for![39]

The practising of meditation and the like be left to be done in the next life! Let this body go in the service of others..."[40]

Religion in his view was a means to reach the God. But the God was not in temples. There was no need to worship any image:

"This is the gist of all worship—to be pure and to do good to others. He who sees Siva in the poor, in the weak, and in the diseased, really worship Siva; and if he sees Siva in the image, his worship is but preliminary. He, who has served and helped one poor man seeing Siva in him, without thinking of his caste, or creed or race, or anything, with him Siva is more pleased than, with the man who sees Him only in the temples."[41]

He questioned monks:

"But what have we, several millions of sanyasins, been doing for the masses? Teaching them metaphysics! That is all madness...[42]

If you want any good to come, just throw your ceremonial overboard and worship the living God, the Man-God—every being that wears a human form... Neither it is work to cogitate as to wether the rice-plate should be placed in front of God for ten minutes or for half an hour that is called lunacy. Millions of rupees have been spent only that the temple-doors at Varanasi or Virindaban may play at opening and shutting all day long! Now the Lord is having His toilet, now he is tak-

But what have we, several millions of sanyasins, been doing for the masses? Teaching them metaphysics! That is all madness...

39. Datta, p-285-86.
40. Ibid.,
41. *Lectures From Colombo to Almora*, p-44.
42. C.W. Vol-VI, 1956, p-264.

ing His meal, now He is busy on something else...And all this, while the living God is dying for want of food, for want of education! The baniyas of Bombay are erecting hospitals for bugs—while they do nothing for men even if they die! You have not the brain to understand this simple thing—that it is a plague with our country, and lunatic asylums are rife all over...Let some of you spread like fire and preach this worship of the universal aspect of the Godhead.."[43]

He asked his brother-monks to give up the religion they were studying and preaching so far. The need of the time was a new religion:

"We want a religion which will give us faith in ourselves, a national self-respect and a power to feed and educate the poor and relieve the misery around us"[44]

When one of his gurubhais confronted him saying that he was not preaching Sri Ramakrishna and instead of bhakti and Sadhna, he was asking his disciples to go about work, serving the poor and the diseased, the Swami thundered:

"What do you know? You are an ignorant man... What do you understand of religion? You are only good at praying with folded hands, 'O Lord! How beautiful is your nose! How sweet are your eyes! And all such nonsense...As if He is such a fool as to make himself a praying thing in the hand of imbecile."[45]

He remarked:

"Your Bhakti is sentimental nonsense, which makes one impotent. Who cares for Bhakti or Mukti? Who cares what the scriptures say? I will go into a thousand hells cheerfully, if I can rouse my countrymen, immersed in tomes, to stand on their own feet and be men inspired with the spirit of Karma Yoga. I am not a follower of Ramakrishna or anyone I am a follower of

Your Bhakti is sentimental nonsense, which makes one impotent. Who cares for Bhakti or Mukti? Who cares what the scriptures say? I will go into a thousand hells cheerfully, if I can rouse my countrymen, immersed in tomes, to stand on their own feet and be men inspired with the spirit of Karma Yoga. I am not a follower of Ramakrishna or anyone I am a follower of him only who serves and help others without his own Bhakti or Mukti.

43. Ibid., p-265.
44. Ibid.,
45. Swami Nikhlananda, *Swami Vivekananda-A Biography*, Calcutta, 1970, p-128.

him only who serves and help others without his own Bhakti or Mukti."[46]

He said further:

"If you seek your own salvation, you will go to hell. It is the salvation of others that you must seek...and even if you have to go to hell in working for others, that is worth more than to gain heaven by seeking your own salvation....Believe me, from the shedding of our life-blood will arise gigantic, heroic workers and warriors of God who will revolutionise the world."[47]

He instructed one of his disciples, KS Ramaswami Shastri:

"Let no one talk of Karma, if it was their Karma to suffer, it is our Karma to relieve their sufferings. If you want to find God, serve man. To reach Narayna you must serve the Daridranaryana—the starving millions of India."[48]

So much was his concern for the masses that he often rebuked the youngsters for not doing their duties towards their country and countrymen. Once he got infuriated at a gentleman from Punjab who came to hear his spiritual lecture. In those days Punjab was near famine. Instead of giving a lecture on religion, Vivekananda spoke on the ways and means of providing relief to the suffering masses. To the visitor it was a wasted visit. When he expressed his disappointment, Vivekananda told him angrily:

"Sir, so long as even a dog of my country remains without food, to feed and take care of him is my religion and anything else is either non-religion or false religion.[49]

"What will you do with a Mahatma residing some-where in the Himalayas and appearing before you from the sky when the people around you are dying of star-

46. Datta, p-321.
47. Romain Rolland p-146.
48. Life Vol-I, p-338, 1979.
49. C.W. Vol-II, 1970, p-782.

vation and the millions are degenerating for the want of education? Nonsense! If you want to find God, serve man."[50]

His feelings were expressed in the poem, "The Living God":

> *"He who is in you and outside you,*
> *Who works through all hands,*
> *Who walks on all feet, whose body is all ye,*
> *Him worship and break all other idols*
> *Again he wrote;*
> *"Ye fools! Who neglect the living God,*
> *And His infinite reflection, with which the world is full,*
> *While ye run after imaginary shadows,*
> *That lead alone to fights and quarrels,*
> *Him worship, the only visible! Break all other idols!*[51]

The widespread education and the consequent awareness and better conditions of the masses in the west convinced him that until and unless Indian masses too are equipped with the power of knowledge, they would not be able to work towards their salvation and the desired change in the system. In numerous letters written to his brother monks and disciples, Vivekananda emphasised the need for education. When he came back to India, he pinpointed the drawbacks of the then existing educational system and the need for the education that could make man self-confident, self-reliant, strong, spiritual and secular.

He explained in his lectures, addresses and articles, that the chief cause of India's ruin had been the monopolizing of education and intelligence by a handful of men.[52] Though the new education introduced by the British was open for everyone yet it

50. Life. Vol-I, p-213.
51. Datta, p-285-86.
52. C.W. Vol-VI, 1956, p-415.

was in the reach of only a few, besides it was confined to cities only whereas the masses lived in villages. Criticising the education that was being imparted in schools and colleges, Vivekananda stated that it was making Indians a race of dyspeptics:

"Education is not the amount of information that is put into your brain and run-riot there, undigested all your life. We must have life-building, man-making, character-making assimilation of ideas.[53]

"The education that does not help the common mass of the people to equip themselves for the struggle for life, which does not bring out strength of character, a spirit of philanthropy, and the courage of lion—is it worth the name? Real education is that which enables one to stand on one's own legs"[54]

A few hundred modernised, half educated and de-nationalised men are all the show of modern english India—nothing else. Castigating such educated Indians, he said:

"You are thinking yourselves highly educated. What nonsense have you learnt. Getting by heart the thoughts of others in foreign language and stuffing your brain with them and taking some university degrees, you consider yourselves educated! Fie upon you! Is this education? What is the goal of your education? Either a clerkship, or being a rougish lawyer, or at the most a Deputy Magistracy, which is another form of clerkship—isn't that all? What good it will do you or the country at large? Open your eyes and see what a piteous cry for food is rising in the land of Bharta, proverbial for its wealth! Will your education fulfil this want? Never."[55]

At another place, he echoed the same:

"...Promenading the sea-shores with books in your hands—repeating undigested stray bits of European

...Promenading the sea-shores with books in your hands—repeating undigested stray bits of European brainwork, and the whole soul bent upon getting a thirty rupees clerkship or at best becoming a lawyer– the height of young India's ambition and every student with a whole brood of hungry children crackling at his heels and asking for bread! Is there not water enough in the sea to drown you, books, gowns, university diplomas and all?

---

53. C.W. Vol-III, 1948, p-302.
54. C.W. Vol-VII, 1947, p-145.
55. Ibid., p-180.

brainwork, and the whole soul bent upon getting a thirty rupees clerkship or at best becoming a lawyer—the height of young India's ambition and every student with a whole brood of hungry children crackling at his heels and asking for bread! Is there not water enough in the sea to drown you, books, gowns, university diplomas and all?[56]

Do you feel for others? If you do not feel for others, you may be the most intellectual giant ever born, but you will be nothing, you are but dry intellect."[57]

In his article 'India and Her Problems', the Swami rebuked such educated:

"So long as the millions live in hunger and ignorance, I hold every man a traitor, who having been educated at their expense, pays not the least heed to them! I call those men who strut about in their finery, having got all their money by grinding the poor wretches, so long as they do not do anything for those two hundred millions who are now no better than hungry savages!"[58]

He declared, "…We must have the whole education of our country, spiritual and secular, in our own hands and it must be on national lines, through national methods as far as practical."[59]

He was well aware of the hold religion had over the masses, hence he suggested that secular education be taught through the medium of religion. He chose Sanyasins and the dedicated youth as teachers to impart education to the masses. He told the Sanyasins that they had a duty towards the masses:

"There are thousands of single-minded, self-sacrificing Sanyasins in our country going from village to village, teaching religion. If some of them can be organised as teachers of secular things also, they will go from place to place, from door to door, not only

56. Letters, p-64.
57. See for detail Vivekanada's lecture on *'Practical Vedanta'*.
58. C.W. Vol-V, 1947, p-45.
59. *Lectures from Colombo to Almora*, p-227.

preaching but teaching also. Suppose two of these men go to a village in the evening with a camera, a globe, some maps etc. they can teach a great deal of astronomy and geography to the ignorant. By telling stories about different nations, they can give the poor, a hundred times more information through the ear than they can get in a lifetime through the books."[60]

He diagnosed that the root cause of illiteracy was poverty. By the end of the nineteenth century, ninety-eight per cent of our population was illitrate. Children of the poor men could not go to school, on growing up they worked with their parents in the fields or factories. Hence Vivekananda advocated a novel idea:

"Now if the Mountain does not come to Mohammed, Mohammed must go to the Mountain. If the poor boy cannot come to education, education must go to them.[61]

...My plans are, therefore, to reach these masses of India. Suppose you start schools all over India for the poor. Still you cannot educate them. How can you? The boys of four years would better go to the plough or to work than to schools...If a ploughman's boy cannot come to education why not meet him at the plough, at the factory, just wherever he is? Go along with him like his shadow.[62]

Go to their cottages, from door to door, in the evening, at noon, anytime, and open their eyes."[63]

He advocated not equal but greater opportunities and financial facilities for the children of Shudras as the Brahmin born clever could educate himself:

"If there is inequality in nature, still there must be equal chance for all—or if greater for some and for some less—the weaker should be given more chance than the strong. In other words, a Brahmin is not so

60. C.W. Vol-IV, 1948, p-309.
61. Ibid., p-308
62. C.W. Vol-VIII, p-89, 1959.
63. C.W. Vol-VI, p-386-87.

much in need of education as a Chandala. If the son of a Brahmin needs one teacher, that of Chandala needs ten.[64]

... if the Brahmin has more aptitude for learning on the ground of heredity than the Pariah, spend no more money on the Brahmin's education, but spend all on the Pariah. Give to weak, for there the entire gift is needed. If the Brahmin is born clever he can educate himself without help. If the others are not born clever let them have all the teaching and the teachers they want. This is justice and reason as I understand it."[65]

In his scheme of education, the poor stood first and the rest afterwards. When one of his Gurubhai, Swami Akhandananda opened a school at Bhagalpore and informed Vivekananda who at that time was in California, the latter wrote back:

"The starting of a centre at Bhagalpore that you have written about is no doubt a good idea—enlightening the school boys and things of that sort but our mission is for the destitute, the poor and the illiterate peasantry and labouring classes and if after everything has been done for them first, there is spare time, then only for the gentry."[66]

I am born to organise these youngmen; nay hundred more in every city are ready to join me; and I want to send them rolling like irresistible waves over India, bringing comfort, morality, religion, education to the doors of the meanest and the most down-trodden. And this I will do or die.

He was so keen and ethusiastic to spread education among the masses that he had chalked out a plan in this context within one-year of his reaching America. From his letters, it seems that he had also got some youngmen to work out his plan in India. On January 29, 1894, he wrote a letter to Haridas Viharidas Desai:

"I am born to organise these youngmen; nay hundred more in every city are ready to join me; and I want to send them rolling like irresistible waves over India, bringing comfort, morality, religion, education to the doors of the meanest and the most down-trodden. And this I will do or die."[67]

---

64. Ibid. p-319.
65. C.W. Vol-III, 1947, p-193.
66. C.W. Vol-VI, p-427, 1956.
67. *Life*, Vol-I, p-533.

Later, Gandhi adopted this phrase during the Quit India Movement.

Vivekananda was a man of rare intellect and was much ahead of his times. He emphasised the need for technical education which could create jobs and was essential for the development of the Indian industry. He denounced the compradore activity of the Indian bourgeoisie associated with the colonial rulers and rebuked them for not establishing their own industries. As far back as in 1890's Vivekananda said about the big Marwari merchant:

"They have the little understanding of their own interest. If the money that they lay out in their business (trade) and with which they make only a small percentage of profit, were utilized in conducting a few factories and workshops instead of filling the pockets of Europeans by letting them reap the benefit of most of transactions, then it would not only conduce to the well-being of the country but bring the far greater amount of profit to themselves as well."[68]

He advised them:

"With the help of western sciences set yourselves to dig the earth and produce foodstuffs—not by means of mean servitude of others—but by discovering new avenues to production, by your own exertions aided by western sciences."[69]

It is said that during his first voyage to USA, Vivekananda happened to meet Jamshedji Tata who was sailing on the same ship. Vivekananda talked about the drain of wealth from India, and tried to convince Tata of the supreme need for India's industrialization. He also advised Tata not to import matches from Japan, but to set up a match factory in India itself, which would help him earn a larger profit and at the same time provide employment for many of his countrymen and check the drain of wealth from India.[70]

> With the help of western sciences set yourselves to dig the earth and produce foodstuffs—not by means of mean servitude of others—but by discovering new avenues to production, by your own exertions aided by western sciences.

68. C.W. Vol-V, 1947, p-283.
69. Ibid, Vol-VII, 1947, p-181.
70. Jayshree Mukherjee, *The Ramakrishna-Vivekananda Movement*, Farma KLM, 1997, p-142.

He also suggested that Tata open an Indian University to provide scientific knowledge. Tata gave the idea a serious thought and wrote back to Vivekananda on 23 November, 1898:

"I very much recall at this moment your views on the growth of the ascetic spirit in India, and the duty, not of destroying, but of diverting it into useful channels. I recall these ideas in connection with my scheme of a research institute of science in India...It seems to me that no better use can be made of the Ascetic spirit than the establishment of monastries or resedential halls for men dominated by the spirit, where they should live with ordinary decency, and devote their lives to the cultivation of science—natural and humanistic."[71]

Initially, Vivekananda himself had tried to bring change through an armed revolt by seeking support of the native princes, failing which he decided to go abroad and raise money for awakening the Indian masses.

The Parliament of Religions, at Chicago was not the main object when the young devotees at Madras began to collect subscriptions for sending him to the Parliament as a delegate. Vivekananda told them that he might not attend the Parliament at all.[72]

As a matter of fact, he did not carry out even the formalities required for selection as a delegate to the Parliament. Before his departure to the United States, he said to his brother monk Haribhai, at the Abu Station:

"I have now travelled all over India, and lately Maharastra...and the western coast. But alas! It was an agony to me, my brother to see with my own eyes the terrible poverty and misery of the masses, and I could not restrain my tears! It is now my firm conviction that it is futile to preach religion amongst them without first trying to remove their poverty and their sufferings. It is

---

71. Eckehard Kulke, *The Parsees in India*, Vikas, N.D. 1974, p-258.
72. C.W. Vol-VII, 1947, p-468.

for this reason—to find some means for the salvation of the poor in India—that I am now going to America."[73]

He said further:

"Haribhai, I am still unable to understand anything of your so called religion. But my heart has expanded very much and I have learnt to feel (the suffering of others) Believe me, I feel intensely indeed."[74]

He revealed his plan:

"I shall now cross the ocean and go to the western nations in the name of India's millions. There I shall earn money by the power of my brain and returning to my country devote myself to carry out my plans for their regeneration or die in the attempt."[75]

Writing to Haripada Mitra, one of his disciples, from Chicago:

"I came to this country not to satisfy my curiosity, not for the name or fame, but to see if I could find any means for the support of the poor in India. If God helps me, You will know gradually what those means are..."[76].

His own countrymen had failed him and that is why he had made up his mind to raise funds in foreign countries. In a letter written to one of his disciples, he explained:

"I travelled in search of funds, but do you think people of India were going to spend money! Selfishness personified—are they to spend money on anything. Therefore I have come to America, to earn money myself and then to return to my country and devote the rest of my days to the realisation of this one aim of my life."[77]

His letter to Ala Singa written on August 20, 1893 echoed the same anguish:

> I came to this country not to satisfy my curiosity, not for the name or fame, but to see if I could find any means for the support of the poor in India. If God helps me, You will know gradually what those means are...

---

73. *Life* Vol-I, p-141.
74. *Letters*, p-76.
75. *Life*-Vol-II, p-203.
76. *Letters*, p-80.
77. C.W. VI, 1956, p-255.

Feel for the
miserable and look
up for help...I have
travelled twelve
years with this load
in my heart and this
idea in my head. I
have gone from
door to door of the
so-called rich and
great. With a
bleeding heart I
have crossed half
the world to this
strange land,
seeking help.

"Feel for the miserable and look up for help...I have travelled twelve years with this load in my heart and this idea in my head. I have gone from door to door of the so-called rich and great. With a bleeding heart I have crossed half the world to this strange land, seeking help."[78]

Numerous letters of Vivekananda written to his disciples speak of his efforts to raise funds for the upliftment of his people. He remained there for four years and did not come back immediately after the Parliament of Religions was over.

"I may parish of cold or hunger in this land, but I bequeath to you, youngman, this sympathy, this struggle for the poor, the ignorant, the oppressed. First I will try in America: and if I fail, try in England."[79]

His concern and his zeal for raising the masses was unexhaustive. He exhorted all those he knew, to work in the same direction. He asked Ala Singa to urge the Raja of Ramnad with whom the former had intimate relations, and other rich men to sympathise with the masses of India. "Tell them" he wrote on November, 2, 1893, "how they are standing on the neck of the poor and that they are not fit to be called men if they don't try to raise them up."[80]

In a letter written on 24 January, 1894, to one of his disciples from Madras, Vivekananda wrote that the fate of the nation depends upon the condition of the masses. He asked:

"Can you raise them? Can you give them back their lost individuality..? Onward forever! Sympathise for the poor, the downtrodden, even unto death—this is our motto."[81]

He did not deviate from the mission he had set for himself even for a moment. His letter written to Ramakrishnananda on March 19, 1894 speaks of the

78. C.W. Vol-V, 1947, p-14.
79. Ibid., p-14.
80. *Letters*, p-76.
81. C.W. Vol-V, p-14.

height of his patriotism and his compassion for his countrymen.

"I shall try to earn the wherewithal myself to the best of my might, and carry out my plans or die in the attempt. When death is certain, it is best to sacrifice oneself for a good cause."[82]

As lecturing was a very profitable occupation, he stayed back to earn money. Even in the World Parliament of Religion, he spoke on "Religion Not the Crying Need of India" in which he commented on the fact that it was not religion of which the Indians stood in need, but bread. He also stated that what had brought him to the west was to seek aid for his impoverished people.[83]

"You Christians who are so fond of sending out missionaries to save the souls of heathens, why do you not try to save their bodies from starvation?...you erect churches all through India, but the crying evil in the east is not religion—they have religion enough and more than they need—but it is bread that these suffering millions of burning India cry out for with parched throats."[84]

He appealed to send missionaries to India to teach them how better to earn a piece of bread and not teach their 'metaphysical nonsense.'Even in his lectures and private conversations, he constantly asked the Americans to send to India instructors in industry. The 'Salem, Evening News' (US) reported:

"The speaker (Swami) explained his mission in this country to be to organize monks for industrial purposes, that they might give the people the benefit of this industrial education and thus elevate and improve their condition."[85]

Lucy Monroe endorses the same. According to her: "His original purpose in coming to this country (US)

82. C.W. Vol-VI, 1956, p-225.
83. *Life*. Vol-I, p-424, 1979.
84. C.W. Vol-I, 1947, p-21.
85. G.S. Banhatti, p-220.

was to interest Americans in the starting of the new industries among the Hindoos (Indians)."[86]

All this makes it clear that his visit had nothing to do with spreading of religion but an opportunity to work for the regeneration of his people from foreign land as the rich of his own motherland had failed him. In United States and later in England he appealed to the rich and worked himself to earn some money through lectures. He tried to know the steps that had take them ahead of the rest of the world. He found that it were education, organization, lack of jealousy, unity, obedience and faith in oneself.

On his return to India, he sets himself enthusiastically to the task of raising the masses. Through his lectures, addresses, conversations and writings, he brought a storm in the thinking and action of many of the patriots. His exhortations, which came straight from his heart, caused stir and successfully set the youth, whom he had chosen as his co-workers, to work for the elevation of the masses. KS Ramaswami, who heard his first lecture in Madras, 'My Plan of Campaign' writes in his reminiscences:

"I felt thrilled to the innermost core of my being by his words and my eyes were wet with tears. Many others who heard the speech were in the same predicament. Then and there some of us took a vow to do what we could to relieve the ignorance, poverty, and misery of the masses of India to the extent possible for each one of us."[87]

He asked Ala Singa to train a band of fiery youngmen. "Put your fire in them and gradually increase the organization letting it widen and widen its circle. Do the best you can. Do not wait to cross the river when the water has all run down. You must have a hold on the masses.[88]

---

86. C.W. III, 1948, p-447.
87. *Reminiscences....* p-104.
88. *Letters*, p-103.

"Go and preach to all, 'Arise, Awake, Sleep no more; within each of you there is the power to remove all wants and miseries. Believe this and that power will be manifested."[89]

He condemned the way the hindu society disowned Buddha's message:

"The Lord once came to you as Buddha and taught you how to feel, how to sympathise with the poor, the miserable the sinner, but you heard Him not. Your priests invented the horrible story that the Lord was here for deluding demons with false doctrines.[90]

Who cares whether there is heaven or a hell, who cares if there is a soul or not, who cares if there is an unchangeable or not. Here is the world, and it is full of misery. Go out into it as Buddha did, and struggle to lessen it or die in the attempt. Forget yourselves; is the first lesson to be learnt, whether you are a theist or an atheist, whether you are agonistic or a Vedantist, a Christian or a Mohammedan."[91]

He asked the youth to awaken the 'Sleeping Leviathan', i.e., who when realised would blow off the oppression.[92] Masses require new ideas and the duty of the patriots should be to "put the chemical together, the crystallization comes in the law of nature. Our duty is to put the ideas into their heads, they will do the rest."[93]

During the last years of his life, he told his disciples:

"Now my one desire is to rouse the country—the sleeping leviathan that has lost all faith in his power and makes no responses.

Mukti and all else appear of no consequences to me.[94]

89. C.W. Vol-VI, 1956, p-454.
90. *Life* Vol-I, 1979, p-526.
91. C.W. Vol-II, 1970, p-353.
92. C.W. Vol-VI, 1956, p-381.
93. C.W. Vol-IV, 1948, p-308.
94. C.W. Vol-VII, 1947, p-186.

"Push on with the organization...It is life to do good, it is death not to do good to others...Feel my children, feel for the poor, the ignorant, the downtrodden; feel till the heart stops and the brain reels and you think you will go mad.[95]

First go down to the very bottom of thing, to the very root of the matters...Put the fire there and let it burn upwards and make an Indian nation."[96]

To him political liberation without economic justice was meaningless. He was critical of the Indian National Congress which was mainly representing the interest of the upper classes and not of the starving millions, the workers and the peasants. "Remember that the nation lives in cottage" he told the Indian patriots. "No amount of politics would be of any avail until the masses in India are once more well educated, well fed and well cared for. If we want to regenerate India we must work for them."[97]

The concern for Indian masses remained the central point of all his activities.While addressing a gathering of young men at Lahore, he said:

"Young men of Lahore...you may make thousands of societies, twenty thousand political assemblages, fifty thousand institutions. These will be of no use until there is that sympathy, that love, that heart that thinks for all....[98]

Give up this little life of yours. What matters is if you die of starvation—you and I and thousand like us—so long as the nation lives? The nation is sinking, the curse of unnumbered millions is on our heads—those to whom we have been giving ditch water to drink when they have been dying of thirst and while the perennial river of water was following past, the unnumbered millions whom we have allowed to starve in the sight of plenty....Wipe of this blot. 'Arise and awake' What

95. C.W. Vol-IV, 1948, p-367.
96. C.W. Vol-III, p-221.
97. C.W. Vol-V, 1947, p-110.
98. C.W. Vol-III, 1948, p-430.

matters if this little life goes? Everyone has to die, the saint or the sinner, the rich or the poor. The body never remains for anyone. Arise and awake and be perfectly sincere. Our insincerity in India is awful; what we want is character, that steadiness and character that make a man cling on to a thing like grim death.[99]

Arise and awake, for the time is passing and all our energies will be frittered away in vain talking. Arise and awake, let minor things and quarrels over little details and fights over little doctrines be thrown aside, for there is the greatest of all works, here are the sinking millions.[100]

Work as if on each of you depended the whole work. Fifty centuries are looking on you, the future of India depends on you. Work on."[101]

His words spell a magic. At Lahore, a large number of B.A. students, who had a long talk with the Swami, immediately formed an association of entirely unsectarian character, as suggested, for work among the poor, the Daridranarayana.[102]

He explained:

"What we (present-day Indians) have not, perhaps did not exist in the past (India) What the Yavanas possessed, by the life-breath of which tremendous forces generated in the electric battery of Europe are encompassing the whole world, that is wanted. That exertion is wanted, that love of independence, that self reliance, that immovable fortitude, that practality, that bond of unity that thirst for progress. Postponing for a while the eternal-looking-backwardness, the infinite all embracing forward look is wanted, and is wanted Rajguna (the priciple of activity) flowing from every nerve from head to foot.."[103]

---

99. C.W. Vol-III, p-431.
100. Ibid., p-432.
101. C.W. Vol-IV 1948, p-370.
102. *Vivekananda in Indian Newspapers*, p-562.
103. C.W. IV, 1948, p-337.

Arise and awake, for the time is passing and all our energies will be frittered away in vain talking. Arise and awake, let minor things and quarrels over little details and fights over little doctrines be thrown aside, for there is the greatest of all works, here are the sinking millions.

What we (present-day Indians) have not, perhaps did not exist in the past (India) What the Yavanas possessed, by the life-breath of which tremendous forces generated in the electric battery of Europe are encompassing the whole world, that is wanted. That exertion is wanted, that love of independence, that self reliance, that immovable fortitude, that practality, that bond of unity that thirst for progress. Postponing for a while the eternal-looking-backwardness, the infinite all embracing forward look is wanted, and is wanted Rajguna (the priciple of activity) flowing from every nerve from head to foot..

Despite his ill-health, Vivekananda made a tour of Dacca in 1901 and there he advised the revolutionaries and the common people to fight not only for political liberation but also for economic justice, for the service of the poor, the downtrodden, the suppressed oppressed and the repressed masses.[104]

His passionate speeches chalked out the path for many of the patriots who clubbed their political struggle with the establishment of an egalitarian society. The Indian revolutionary struggle thus owes its orientation to the left to Vivekananda. During the last days of his life, when Vivekananda remained confined to his *Math* at Belure, he used to advise, the students who visited him in large numbers for his blessings: "What good is there if you practice Yoga, while your brothern die of starvation. Go help the needy; succour the poor and make country a honeycomb, as it were."[105] Expressing the hope that the future belonged to the masses and it was not a distant destiny, He said:

"The masses of Europe and America have been the first to awaken and have already begun the fight, signs of this awakening have shown themselves in India, too, as is evident from the number of the strikes among the lower classes nowadays. The upper classes will no longer be able to repress the lower, try they ever so much... Therefore I say, set yourselves to the task of spreading education among the masses...Kindle their knowledge with the help of the modern science."[106]

Thus, like Karl Marx, Vivekananda was against exploitation, oppression and injustice in the society. He condemned the upper classes as well as the priestly class for keeping the people illiterate, ignorant and poverty ridden. He believed in equality and was for equal opportunities for all. He was against the concentration of economic power in the hands of few and regarded the western democracy a farce. He predicted the rule of

104. Datta, p-334.
105. Manmohan Ganguly, *Swami Vivekananda-A Study*, Contemporary Pub. Calcutta, 1907, p-63.
106. Ibid., Vol-VII, 1947, p-146-47.

Shudras i.e., the downtrodden in India in the future and advocated socialism.

Though he did not regard it as the perfect system, yet he was in favour of it as other systems were for the rich classes. He said:

"Let this one be tried—if for nothing else, for the novelty of the thing. A redistribution of pain and pleasure is better than always the same person having pains and pleasure."[107]

But unlike Marx, he did not regard religion as opium. Godless socialism was not acceptable to him. He said:

"Everything goes to show that socialism or some form of rule by the people, call it what you will, is coming on the board. The people will certainly want the satisfaction of their material needs less work, no oppression, no war, and more food. What guarantee have we that this or any civilization will–last, unless it is based on religion, on the goodness of man? Depend on it, religion goes to the root of the matter. If it is right, all is right."[108]

Socialism with Spiritualism was his philosophy.

There is yet another fundamental difference between the two in their concept of socialism. Vivekananda's socialism provides ample freedom to the individual for his growth. 'Freedom is the only condition of growth; take that off, the result is degeneration'. Marx's socialism lacks this freedom as it emphasizes over centralized society.

Besides, he had no faith in the materialistic interpretation of history and did not believe in the class war. He did not favour classless society and was against the abolition of the feudal lords, the princes and the rich classes. He specifically advised his disciples to take care not to set up class strife between the poor peasants, the labouring people and wealthy classes. He wanted to

---

107. C.W. Vol-VI, 1956, p-381.
108. C.W. Vol-V, 1947, p-51.

My noble Prince! The life is short, the vanities of the world transient, but they alone live who live for others, the rest are more dead than alive. One such high, noble-minded, and royal son of India as Your Highness, can put it on its feet again, and then leave a name to the posterity, which shall be worshipped as god. May the Lord make your noble heart feel intensely for the suffering millions of India sunk in ignorance, is the prayer of Vivekananda.

The first and the foremost task in India is the propagation of education and spirituality among the masses. It is impossible for hungry men to be spiritual, unless food is provided for them. Hence our paramount duty lies in showing them new ways of food supply.

change by changing the hearts of the exploiters, with the power of love, the method, later followed by Gandhi. In a letter to the Maharaja of Mysore, Vivekanand made an appeal:

"My noble Prince! The life is short, the vanities of the world transient, but they alone live who live for others, the rest are more dead than alive. One such high, noble-minded, and royal son of India as Your Highness, can put it on its feet again, and then leave a name to the posterity, which shall be worshipped as god. May the Lord make your noble heart feel intensely for the suffering millions of India sunk in ignorance, is the prayer of Vivekananda."[109]

The Raja of Khetri, Ajit Singh, under the influence of Vivekananda took steps to provide relief to his subjects but unfortunately had an accident and died prematurely.

Thus Vivekananda's way of bringing change was different from the Marxist. He believed in evolution and not revolution. Education was the way, youth and the sanyasins the forces to work out the transition towards a socialistic state. The establishment of the Ramakrishna Mission was also a step in the same direction. Service for the poor and the needy was the mission of the *Math*. The rules of the *Math* provided: "The first and the foremost task in India is the propagation of education and spirituality among the masses. It is impossible for hungry men to be spiritual, unless food is provided for them. Hence our paramount duty lies in showing them new ways of food supply."[110]

He did not only preach, he lived every moment of his life to serve Daridra who was his Narayna. His compassion transmitted to his disciples too. In the summer of 1897 during famine in Murshidabad district of Bengal, Vivekanand's disciples fed the suffering poor people for about five months. Abandoned

109. *Letters*, p-113.
110. *The Indian Renaissance Ramakrishna and Vivekananda* p-63.

children were collected and an orphanage at Mohura was opened where along with education, the children were taught the trade of weaving, tailoring etc. He instructed his disciples:

"Curtail the expenses on worship to a rupee or two per mensem. The children of the God are dying of starvation. Worship with water and Tulsi alone, and let the allowances on Bhoga (food-offering) be sent in offering food to the living God who dwells in the person of poor..."[111]

In 1898 when plague broke out, Vivekanand put himself at the head of the relief work. Under his instructions, the students organised themselves to inspect the houses of the poor and to provide relief. He ordered his Sanyasin disciples to sell the monasteries:

"Sell it, if necessary. We are Sanyasins, we ought always to be ready to sleep under the trees and live on what we beg every day."[112]

He himself came to live in a poor locality to inspire courage in the people and cheer up the workers. Gandhiji later followed Vivekananda and lived in Harijan localities.

His entire life was a supreme dedication for the cause he held dearest—the raising of the masses. With undaunted courage, he relentlessly worked to fulfill the vow he had taken at Kanyakumari. Though he could not succeed in his mission, yet the path shown by him led many of our freedom fighters to combine the struggle for political liberation with economic justice. Thus Vivekananda can be called as the precursor of all the leftist movements in India.

111. C.W. Vol VI, 1956, p-405.
112. Romain Rolland, p-132.

Conclusion

The life story of Swami Vivekananda is the saga of his relentless efforts against India's enslavement, social degradation, spiritual decadence and economic exploitation. His life was very short but the power released was enormous. It created a revolution in the world of thought and action. Whether it were freedom fighters, social reformers, writers or philosophers, all were drawn towards his magnetic personality and teachings. They were awakened, aroused, inspired and set to work for the regeneration of their motherland.

Born and brought up in a liberal atmosphere and well equipped with modern education, he became a monk by choice. The two separate phases of his life did not clash but made a unique combination, which makes Vivekananda stand apart from all other saints, philosophers and freedom fighters.

Vivekananda's nature was not to submit to any dominance. Naturally, the domination of the country by the British colonialists agitated him. He pondered over and found that the main reason for the downfall of India was social and religious decadence of the hindus and the real culprit was the Brahmin, particularly the priestly class which in order to maintain its hegemony over the rest had enslaved the society by misinterpreting and misrepresenting the religion. He called them crackbrains, greedy, selfish and responsible for the all round backwardness of the country and asked the people to be men and kick out priests who are always against progress.

He disagreed with the view that four major castes were the creation of Brahma. He was the first to say that caste was a social institution, invented by the priestly class and had nothing to do with religion. Without demolishing the caste system, he emphasized over caste mobility i.e., one could change caste by acquiring the needed virtues. A Shudra could become a Brahmin and be entitled to all the rights, including the study of Vedas and preaching the Hindu religion. In order to give Shudras their due place in the society, Vivekananda suggested not equal but more opportunities and all state assistance in independent India and none for the upper castes as they were capable. He stood for close interaction among all hindus including the Shudras and advocated inter-dining and inter-caste marriages. Those who own him today spared no words in maligning and abusing a great dalit leader Baba Saheb Ambedkar when the latter married a Brahmin woman.

He belied the argument that the muslims were responsible for the enslavement of the hindu women. He made it bold to say that hindu scripture and Brahmins were responsible for the pitiable state of the women. Without women emancipation and empowerment, Indian society and nation could not progress. Hence, he emphasized upon equality and education for women and change in the attitude of Indian men towards women. Along with bookish education, the women should be taught various arts in schools for self-dependence. He also stated that by mere laws, change could not be ushered in. Women have to come forward to work towards their own salvation. More than half a century has passed, yet independent India has not ensured equality to women. Today Indian women are fighting their own battle, to establish a society that Vivekananda had envisaged.

Vivekananda was a modern saint and deviated from many beliefs and practices, which had nothing to do with religion but over the years had been made a part of the religion by the priests. He stood for a social system free from the clutches of the Brahmins. In eating, dressing or any social matters, the individual should be free from the dictates of any authority.

Citing from Shastras, he stated publicly that eating beef was not irreligiousness in ancient times, as the brahmins not only ate beef but also killed the cows.

He was not a revivalist, a charge often made against him. It was first started by the British, probably to keep away the muslims from coming under his influence and joining their hindu brothers in the revolutionary fervour, which had taken Bengal by storm. Sir Valentine Chirole, who came to India as the special correspondent of the London Times in 1907, described him in his book "India Old and New' as an ardent apostle of Hindu revivalism in Bengal. However, a cursory look at his writings makes it crystal clear that he was a die-hard opponent of revivalism and had warned his countrymen to beware of such movements and leaders. He did not advocate going back to Vedas and did not regard Vedas to be the storehouse of all knowledge encompassing all ages. He was critical of some parts of Vedas and asked his followers not to believe them. To look back for building the future would lead to degeneration. He was for a forward look and asked the people not to glorify everything of the past. He wanted Indians to go to foreign countries to learn the modern scientific sciences and to develop India with latest technology. He also assigned a new role to the Indian sanyasins. He suggested that sanyasins, too, should acquire scientific and secular knowledge and impart it, instead of metaphysics, take it to their door steps, their huts, fields and factories.

He was an iconoclastic monk whose God was not in temples and religion not in books. 'God is the creation of man and not man the creation of God' was his belief. To him science was not less important than religion. He used to advice his followers not to believe anything including religion without reasoning. He made it bold to say that all those portions of religious scriptures, which shun reason, should not be believed, Today Vatican City is saying the same thing.

Vivekananda was not a hindu chauvinist. However, by quoting out of context some of his scattered utterances, a few intellectuals as well as politicians have tried to project him so. They call him 'Hindu Napoleon' and an advocate of 'Hindu Rashtra' but the very life and teachings of Vivekananda stand as refutation to such narrow and sectarian creed. Neither his religion nor his nationalism was of the aggressive chauvinistic type. He was proud of the fact that India throughout the long history, was never an aggressor on other's spheres. It was he who stated that all the Indians irrespective of their caste, race, region or religion should say with pride that they are Indians and every Indian is their brother. Though in his speeches made all over the country, he stressed again and again the theme of hindu greatness, however it was not exclusive. As was the norm of the day, Vivekananda too used the words Indian and Hindu interchangeably. According to him all those who lived in the sub-continent were Hindus and the Hindus as a religious community, should call themselves as Vaidikas or Vedantists.

This is also a fact that in pre-independent India, the advocates of Hindu Rashtra did not claim him. On the contrary, they accused him of 'unsaintliness; and doubted his 'sincerity'. Savarkar, who coined the word Hindutva in 1923, did not mention Vivekananda's name in his speeches or writings. Unlike Vivekananda, Savarkar characterized British rule as 'merciful' and cooperated with the Colonialists. Besides, Savarkar was an opponent of Islam and Muslims. He had led a mob in the destruction of a mosque of his village in 1893. Vivekananda respected all religions and was proud of India where hindus built mosques for muslims and churches for the christians.

Today the communalists, who swear by his name, are up in arms for the Ram Temple but their master was against building temples for worship "The living God is within you and yet you are building churches and temples and believing all sorts of imaginary nonsense."

He did not support the cow-protection movement initiated by his predecessor Swami Dayananda and refused to help the cause when approached. The unmeasured veneration for the cow in his opinion was in a great measure responsible for the degeneration of the entire hindu race.

He strongly condemned fanaticism, sectarianism and bigotry and characterized its practitioners as 'lunatics', 'horrible demons', who cause bloodshed of the innocents for their selfish interests. He made it bold to say that the root cause of all religious quarrels is political and economic. The fanatics in order to acquire political power and economic benefits present themselves as the defender of the religion and mislead the masses. Vivekananda asked his followers to accept and follow only those parts of Puranas and Smritis that breathe broadness of spirit and love and rest be rejected.

Besides Vivekananda did not assert the superiority of hinduism over other religions like Swami Dayananda Saraswati or other hindu communalists. According to him all religions were the different ways to reach the same destination. He revered all Sufi saints and the Bhaktas, admired their catholicity and broad outlook and respected their cults. They were all messengers of God and not 'cheat', 'fraud', or ill wishers of hinduism as alleged by Swami Dayananda Saraswati. The communalists quote some of his comments made against Koran and Bible thereby projecting him as anti-Islam and anti-Christianity. However, Vivekananda critically analysed Hinduism too. In fact, he was a very harsh critic of hinduism. He stated that some hindu scriptures were the production of men of low-intelligence and hence should be discarded. He defended Islam in the United States as vigorously as Hinduism.

He was proud of the diversity of his country wherein existed the unity, a uniqueness of India. It was this aspect of India, which he highlighted in his lecture before the World Parliament of Religions, which won him instant popularity and recognition. Other speakers spoke in praise of their countries or the religion they belonged to but Vivekananda emphasized spirituality, which was common to all religions.

Today, in India, anti-conversion laws are being enacted to deny the individual freedom to change his religion. Vivekananda was staunch opponent of any restriction, which curbs the right of freedom in matter of religion. He was against imposition of religion by parents, teachers, or country. According to him man has to be free to accept or reject the religion he was born in. When grown-up the man should select the religion of his choice.

Unlike the hindu communalist, he did not regard the medieval period of India as 'dark ages'. He was aware of the distortion of the Indian history at the hands of the english historians. Hence he asked the Indians to write the Indian history themselves and not to believe in the distorted version. He was proud of India's heritage of harmony which according to him, contributed greatly in making India, a land of prosperity in the medieval period, which dazzled the eyes of the Europeans. He also praised the liberality of the muslim rulers, which had led to the emergence of numerous cults and new religions in India. He explained in his lectures that there never was any religious enmity and every religion was left unmolested by the muslim rulers. He placed the Mughal rulers on a very high pedestal. So much so that he placed Emperor Akbar in the category of Rama and used to shed tears on the defeat of Siraj-ud-daula, the Nawab of Bengal, which had led to the establishment of the East India Company's rule in India. If he was critical of Aurangzeb's rule, he was equally critical of Marratta and Sikh regimes, which came into existence after the downfall of the muslim rule.

Those who regard him as their mentor, charge the muslim rulers for forcible conversion of hindus to Islam. The fact is that Vivekananda regarded muslim rule as a salvation for Shudras. The oppressed and suppressed Shudras for ages at the hands of the

Brahmins, tasted the supper of equality by converting to Islam and later Christianity during the British rule. According to him it was nonsense to say that the sword converted the hindus. Had it been so, the entire Indian population would have been converted to Islam as the muslim rule lasted for almost seven centuries. Besides, he did not regard the muslims as foreigners and put them on equal footing with the hindus. He always addressed the muslims as brothers and did not join the Arya Samaj despite their desperate efforts due to the orthodoxy of the latter. He asked all Indians to unite together against the common enemy not on the basis of religion but on the basis of common oppression.

He spoke with pride about the fact that succession of Imperial rulers born of hindu mothers and muslim fathers was the peculiar genius of Indian civilization. It is worth noting that no hindu obscurantist ever looked with favour on this particular feature of the Medieval Indian history. Vivekananda's admiration for the Islamic component of Indian life did not stop with this particular projection of the past. In his vision of the future too, the ideal Indian would have a muslim body with a Vedantic soul.

Although he was proud of the rich heritage of India's past yet he was equally alive to the necessity of eradicating those evils, which stood as obstacle in the way of its development. However, in foreign lands, he made certain statements, which were far from reality. For instance, he stated in his address that India was a land of religious tolerance and there had never been religious prosecutions, overlooking the suppression of Buddhism by the Brahmins. He was well aware of it and in his lectures, he never made secret of this fact. In United States, he asserted that Hinduism was the best religion but in India, he was a harsh critic of some of its aspects and made it bold to say that Hinduism needs to incorporate some points from other religions, like equality from Islam, activity from Christianity and compassion from Buddhism. Besides, he glorified caste and refuted the argument that Indian widows were denied a decent life. The reason of such assertions can be found in his one sentence 'India with all her faults I love thee still'. He disclosed in his letter, written to Ala Singa in May 1895:

'I am the one man who dared to defend his country and I have given them what they never expected from a Hindu them tit for tat, giving with compound interest.'

He was convinced that freedom couldn't be won by non-violent means. Initially he himself tried to work out an armed revolt and when failed he tried to accomplish his mission by evoking heroic spirit in the youth. He asked them that it was their religious duty to liberate their motherland from the foreign yoke. He often quoted in his lectures Ravana, Arjuna, Nachiketa, Laxmi Bai, Chand Bibi, Satan of Milton, Robert Clive, Chengiz Khan, Alexander and Napoleon to convince them that nothing was impossible. Regeneration of the motherland was more important to him than religion. He wore the saffron garb and used religious terminology to reach the common masses as well as to escape from the suspicion of the British spies. Thus he was an ascetic with a political mission.

His patriotism was greater than any of his contemporaries. When the Congress leaders pledged their loyalty towards the British Crown and did not even dream for self-government, Vivekananda sought and worked for the ouster of the British Colonialists. He was not satisfied with the snail-pace progress of the Indian National Congress. He wanted to reach it with the kick of football. Freedom is everyone's birthright and one has to fight for it if it is suppressed or snatched. Four years after his death, the militants under the leadership of Tilak who was very close to Vivekananda, made an attempt to wrest the leadership of the Congress in their own hands. Tilak was fielded for the presidentship of the Congress in 1906. The moderates could restrain him only by calling back Dada Bhai Nauroji from London but the latter too could not escape the revolutionary fervour produced by Vivekananda's teachings. For the first time, the Congress in its session held in Calcutta 1906, declared Swaraj as its aim.

Vivekananda was for secular India. He felt that different religious ideals should be a matter of personal realization, never being permitted to affect the affairs of the state. It is on this account that he appreciated the Indian National Congress though he was critical of its bourgeois ideology and elitist approach. A mere political change, which was the aim of the Congress and other nationalist forces, was not the desire of Vivekananda. He stood for total change. The words like equality, freedom, and fraternity were not empty words, but the principles on which he wanted to build the future Indian polity as well as society.

He was well aware of the developments taking place all over the world in the realm of thinking and action and interpreted them in terms of their suitability to independent India. During his stay in foreign countries, he had observed the functioning of bourgeois democracy and realized that it was not the rule of the people but of the rich who manipulated to keep the power safely in their own hands and to subjugate the weaker countries for economic exploitation. Thus before Hobson and Lenin, Vivekananda detected the close connection between capitalism and imperialism.

He can be called the precursor of all the left movements and left politics in our country though not given credit by Indian socialists and communists. It was he, who introduced the word socialism in India and gave socialistic direction to our freedom struggle and literature. However his socialism was different from the rest as it incorporated individual freedom and religion, the lack of these two had undoubtedly led to the collapse of the socialist block at the close of the twentieth century. He gave a new meaning to worship. It was not reading, reciting Shastra and serving the idols in the temple but the service of the oppressed and suppressed. By introducing the concept of social service as an integral part of religion and incorporating it as an essential activity of the mission set up by him, he emerges as a great humanist.

An impartial study of Vivekananda convinces that if his ideas had been followed in the pre-independent India by his countrymen, the country would not have been divided and if truly interpreted and applied in the body polity, independent India would have emerged as a truly secular, modern, socialist country, upholding spiritual values with all its inhabitants living in complete harmony, respecting all the religions and contributing their best towards making India once again the wonder of the world.

Bibliography

Ahuja M.L. *Glimpses of Some Great-Indians* Vikas, 1997. N.D.

Atmaprana, Pravarjika, *Sister Nivedita*, Pub-Sister Nivedita's Girl's School, Calcutta, 1961

Atmaprana, Pravrajika, *Swami Vivekananda and Harmony of Religions and Religious Sects* in 'Swami Vivekananda Centenary Memorial Volume; edited by R.C. Majumdar and Swami Sambudhananda, Calcutta, 1963

Athalye, D.V. Swami Vivekananda-The Patriot-Saint, Pub-Ashish N.D. 1979

Amiya Sen, *Swami Vivekananda*, Oxford University Press N.D. 2002.

Arun Chandra Guha, *First Spark of Revolution*, Orient Longman, N.D. 1971.

Atul Chandara Gupta, *Studies in the Bengal Renaissance* National Council of Education, Bengal 1958.

Amiya Sen, *Hindu Revivalism in Bengal,* Oxford University, Press N.D. 1993.

Agnihotri, H.L. *Swami Vivekananda -His Dynamic Vision* Hissar, Pub- Aman publication, 1994.

Amrit Rai, *Premchand-A Life*, PPH, N.D. 1982

Basudha Chakravarty, *Sister Nivedita*, NBT, N.D. 1975

Bandyopadhyay Pranab, *Swami Vivekananda and the Modern World*, United Writers, Calcutta, 1990.

Bagchee Moni *Sister Nivedita*, Pub-Anilchandra Calcutta, 1958

Bannerjee D.N. *India's Nation Builders*, Headley Bros London, 1919

C.S. Subramanyam, *MPT Acharya*, Institute of South Indian Studies, Madras 1995

R.C. Majumdar, History of Bengal, Pub-G. Bhardwaj Calcutta, 1978.

Bhupendra Nath Roy, *Nivedita*, Pub-Mahto West Bengal year of Pub-Not mentioned

Nivedita, Sister, *The Master As I Saw Him*, Udbodhan-office, Calcutta, 1910

Nivedita, Sister, *Swamiji and His Message*, Advaita Ashram Mayavati Himalayas, 1972.

Bhupendranatha Datta, *Swami Vivekananda Patriot-Prophet*, Navabharat Press, Calcutta, 1954.

Selected Essays of Nivedita, Ganesh & Company Madras 1911

Carebanu Cooper, Swami Vivekananda-*Literary Biography*, Bhartiya Vidya Bhavan, Bombay 1984

P. Parameswaram, *Marx and Vivekananda* Sterling N.D. 1987.

V.B. Karnik, M.N. Roy-*Political Biography*, Nav Jagriti Samaj, Bombay, 1978

Binoy Kumar Roy, *Socio-Political Views of Vivekananda* PPH. N.D. 1970

V. K. Rao, *Swami Vivekananda*, Publication Division N.D. 1979

Dayananda Saraswati, *Satyartha Prakash*, (English Trans) by Durga Prasad, Jan Gyan Prakashan N.D. 1970

Talks with Swami Vivekananda- Advaita Ashram, Mayavati, Almora, 1939.

Narayana Bose, *Social Thinking of Swami Vivekananda* Pub-Bina Bose, Lucknow, year of Pub-N.M. V.B. Karnik

Eckhard Kulke, *The Parsees in India*, Vikas, N.D. 1974

Tarachand, *History of Freedom Movement In India* Vol-II.

V.S. Naravane, *Premchand-His Life and Works,* Vikas N.D. 1980

Satyavrata Ghose, *Remembering our Revolutionaries* Marxist Study Forum, Hyderabad, 1999.

Reminiscences of Vivekananda, Eastern & Western Disciples, Advaita, Ashram Publication Dept, Calcutta, 1961

The Life of Swami Vivekananda, Eastern & Western Disciples, Pub-Advaita Ashram, Almora Vol-I & II , 1912, 1913 Rept-1979

Swami Chetnananda ed. *Vedanta-Voice of Freedom*, Advaita Ashram, Calcutta, 1991,

Maharishi Dayananda, *Satyartha Prakash*, (Hindi) Arya Sahitya Prachar Trust, Delhi, 1972.

Vivekananda in Indian Newspapers-1893-02, Extract from 22 Newspapers, ed. Sankri Prasad Basu & Sunil Bihari Ghose, Pub-Bookland, Calcutta, 1969.

Rushbrook Williams, *Great Men of India*, Gian Pub. N.D. 1985

India's Contribution to the World Thought and Culture Pub-Rock Memorial Committee Madras, 1970

R.C. Majumdar, *Swami Vivekananda: A Historical View*, General Pub & Printers Calcutta 1965

R.C. Majumdar, *History of Freedom Movement* Vol-I, Firma K.L. Mukhopadhyay, Calcutta, 1962

Rajgopal Chattopadhyaya, *Swami Vivekananda in India*, Moti Lal Banarsi Das Delhi-1999

Jones J.P., *India-Its Life & Thought*, Rare Books N.D. 1974

J.L. Nehru, *Discovery of India*, Calcutta, Signet 1946

Manmohan Ganguly, *Swami Vivekananda-A Study,* Contemporary Pub, Calcutta, 1907

Santi L. Mukherjee, *The Philosophy of Man-Making,* New Oriental Book Agency, Calcutta, 1971

K. Chattopadhyaya, *Brahmo Samaj Movement*, 1858-83 Papyrus, Calcutta, 1983

Life of Sri Ramakrishna, Compiled from various Authentic sources, Advaita Ashram Almora, 1948.

Nationalistic and Religious Lectures-Retold by Swami Tapsayananda, Advaita Ashram, Calcutta, 1996

Christopher Isherwood, *Ramakrishna and His Disciples*, Advaita Ashram Calcutta, 1965.

Romain Rolland, *The Life of Swami Vivekananda and the Universal Gospel*, Advaita Ashram, Calcutta, 1931.

Swami Tejasananda, *Swami Vivekananda and His Mission*, R.K. Mission, Belur Math 1965

Jyotis Chandra, Das Gupta, *A National Biography for India*, 1911.

K.C. Vyas, D.R. Sardesai, Prof. S.R. Nayak, *India Through the Ages*, Allied Pub. Bombay 1962

Swami Nikhlananda, *Vivekananda-A Biography*, Calcutta 1970

Sanat Kumar Rai Chaudhry, *Swami Vivekananda-The Man and His Mission*, Scientific Book Agency. Calcutta, 1966

Hansraj Rahbar, *Vivekananda-The Warrior Saint*, Forsight Pub. N.D. 1995

Lizelle Reymond, *The Dedicated-Biography of Nivedita*, The John Day Company, New York, 1953

Swami Sat Prakashananda, *Swami Vivekananda's Contribution to the Present Age*. Vedanta Society of St. Louise, America, 1978

Sibanarayan Roy, *Studies in the Bengal Renaissance-First Phase*, Minerva, Associates, Calcutta, 2000

Benishankar Sharma, *Swami Vivekananda-A Forgotton Chapter of His Life*, Calcutta, 1963

Marie Louise Burke, *Swami Vivekananda in America New Discoveries*, Advaita Ashram, Calcutta 1958

Robert D. Baird, ed. *Religions in Modern India*, Manohar, 1989. N.D.

William Radice ed., *Swami Vivekananda and the Modernization of Hinduism*, Oxford University Press, N.D. 1998

Jayshree Mukherjee, The Ramakrishna-Vivekananda Movement, Farma KLM 1997

Last Days of Vivekananda-by Eastern & Western Disciples, Advaita Ashram Calcutta, 1927

Reflections on Swami Vivekananda, ed. by M. Sivaramakrishna, Sterling Pub. N.D. 1993

Notes of Some Wanderings with Swami Vivekananda, ed. S. Sardananda, Pub- Gohendra Nath, Calcutta 1913

Peter Hech, *Nationalism Terrorism, Communalism,* Oxford University Press, Calcutta, 1998

V.D. Savarkar, *Samagra Savarkar Wandmaya,* Vol-VI, Maharastra Prantik Hindu Sabha Poona 1964

Dhananjay Keer, *V.D. Savarkar*, Popular Prakashan Bombay.

Jaykar, M.R. *The Story of My Life*, Asia Publications Bombay 1958

D.S. Sarma, *The Renaissance of Hinduism*, Benaras Hindu University, 1944

Reminiscences of Vivekananda-by Eastern & Western Disciples, Advaita Ashram Calcutta, 1961

I.M. Raisner & N.M. Goldberg ed, *Tilak and the Struggle for Freedom*, PPH, 1966, N.D.

Satish K. Kapoor, *Cultural Contact and Fusion* A.B.S. Pub-1987.

B.K. Ahluwalia, *Vivekananda & Indian Renaissance* Associated, N.D. 1983

Mitra K.N., *Swami Vivekananda*, Vivekananda Society Calcutta, 1913

Nirvednananda, Swami, *Swami Vivekananda, On India And Her Problems* Advaita Ashram, Calcutta, 1971

PRIMARY SOURCES

Vivekananda, Swami, *Lectures From Colombo to Almora*, Advaita Ashram Almora, 1947

Vivekananda, Swami, *Letters of Swami Vivekananda*, Advaita Ashram Almora, 1946

Vivekananda, Swami, *Unpublished Letters of Swami Vivekananda*, Prabudha Bharti, 1950.

Vivekananda, Swami, *Practical Vedanta*, Advaita Ashram, Himalaya 1938.

Vivekananda, Swami, The Complete Works of Swami Vivekananda Advaita Ashram Mayavati Almora Vol-I, 1947.

Vivekananda, Swami, The Comp... Vol-II, 1970

Vivekananda, Swami, The Comp... Vol-III, 1948

Vivekananda, Swami, The Comp... Vol-IV, 1948

Vivekananda, Swami, The Comp... Vol-V, 1947

Vivekananda, Swami, The Comp... Vol-VI, 1956

Vivekananda, Swami, The Comp... Vol-VII, 1947

Vivekananda, Swami, The Comp... Vol-VIII, 1959

Inspired Talks, Advaita Ashram, Almora, 1939 rept 1946

JOURNALS AND MAGAZINES

1. The Modern Review 1922; & 1968, 1969
2. J B R S. [Journal of the Bihar Research Society] 1951 Vol-XXXVII
3. Swami Vivekananda Centenary Celebrations, 1962-63, 1963-64
4. Sunday-31st January 1993 [*Myth About the Swami*] by-Arun Shourie
5. Sunday-*Vision of Hindu India*, 20, May 1993 by D.N. Mishra
6. Frontline-12th March 1993. *A Secular Vivekananda* by Subramanyam
7. Sunday 28 March-3 April 1993 A.R. Bardhan, *Of Shourie and Vivekananda* in
8. The Hindustan Review. Feb. 1903

Index